52 WAYS TO LIVE A

KICK-ASS LIFE

BS-Free Wisdom to Ignite Your Inner Badass and
Live the Life You Deserve

Andrea Owen, CPCC

Adams Media
New York   London   Toronto   Sydney   New Delhi

Aadamsmedia

Adams Media
An Imprint of Simon & Schuster, Inc.
57 Littlefield Street
Avon, Massachusetts 02322

For information about special discounts for bulk purchases, please contact Simon & Schuster Special Sales at 1-866-506-1949 or business@simonandschuster.com.

The Simon & Schuster Speakers Bureau can bring authors to your live event. For more information or to book an event contact the Simon & Schuster Speakers Bureau at 1-866-248-3049 or visit our website at www.simonspeakers.com.

Manufactured in the United States of America

20 19 18 17 16 15 14 13 12

Library of Congress Cataloging-in-Publication Data has been applied for.

ISBN 978-1-4405-6477-2
ISBN 978-1-4405-6478-9 (ebook)

This book is intended as general information only, and should not be used to diagnose or treat any health condition. In light of the complex, individual, and specific nature of health problems, this book is not intended to replace professional medical advice. The ideas, procedures, and suggestions in this book are intended to supplement, not replace, the advice of a trained medical professional. Consult your physician before adopting any of the suggestions in this book, as well as about any condition that may require diagnosis or medical attention. The author and publisher disclaim any liability arising directly or indirectly from the use of this book.

Many of the designations used by manufacturers and sellers to distinguish their products are claimed as trademarks. Where those designations appear in this book and Simon & Schuster, Inc., was aware of a trademark claim, the designations have been printed with initial capital letters.

CONTENTS

ACKNOWLEDGMENTS

To my parents, who gave me an idyllic childhood and have always continued to do the best they can with what they have. To my husband Jason, who met me at a time when I wasn't my best self but was on my way. Your patience, love, and kindness are a gift to me. To my children, Colton and Sydney. Having you both truly lit my fire to be a better person.

To all the strong females whose presence and energy have shaped me: My great-aunt Noel, many of my aunts, my sister Judy, Annamaria Loven, Karina Fidler, Sandee Horan (and her tribe . . . you know who you are), my bestie, Amy Smith—whose wisdom goes years beyond my own and teaches me to be a better woman every day. To Courtney Webster, Carmen Hartmann, and Shelby Christman. To Chris Valdez—an amazing therapist who lovingly called me out on my own BS when I needed it.

And those who made this book possible. My agent, Michele Martin. Thank you for taking a chance on a new author. Adams Media for reaching out to me (!) and believing in my message, voice, and written word. To Jana Scheuberth, Helen House, and Debbie Reber (without you, I would be lost in my self-inflicted author drama).

All my ass-kicking women out there who have followed, inspired, and encouraged me. I write this book for you.

And to my ex-husband. You were the catalyst. Thank you for giving me freedom. And for that, I will be forever grateful.

INTRODUCTION

February 13, 2006

What time will my husband be coming over to my apartment to have dinner on Valentine's Day? I wondered. We were separated at the time, and in limbo about what would happen to our marriage. It was up and down—one day would be great and we'd be talking about working things out, and the next it wasn't looking so good.

I called his cell phone and a woman answered. I had suspected for months he had been having an affair, which was one of the main reasons for our separation. For months he denied it. But the moment she answered his phone, I knew.

I asked her name; she told me.

Without hesitation, I asked her, "Are you sleeping with my husband?" She replied, "If you're asking me that, we need to talk."

At that moment, I knew it was over.

October 2006

I was alone at my soon-to-be ex-husband's parents' house pulling boxes of my things out of their attic. As I walked down the stairs awkwardly carrying a large box, I saw the front doorknob turning. The next second, someone walked in. It was my husband, with his girlfriend in tow. And she was seven months pregnant.

At the time of our separation, we had been discussing conceiving our first child. And here was this woman, standing in front of me, pregnant.

They had a house together and even a dog. And now they were having a baby. Seeing her that day, I wondered if a person could die from heartbreak.

The months that followed were my own proverbial awakening. The world took me by the shoulders and shook the shit out of me. Told me to *Wake the hell up!* I had spent our entire relationship, all thirteen years, suffocating myself. Building a life around someone else because I was simply desperate for love. Was it his fault? No.

I had to take responsibility for the life I had 100 percent participated in creating. On the outside I was happy. But on the inside I was screaming. Convinced something was wrong with me, convinced if only he would change, everything would be great. Perfect, even.

In October 2006, the Universe gave me a one-way ticket to my life. It was up to me to get on board or stay where I was . . . bitter, resentful, blaming, and a victim.

I devoured everything I could to help myself. This book is everything I've learned from my own healing from this incident, plus more.

★

I knew healing wouldn't be easy. In fact, one of my least favorite things to hear is, "That's easier said than done." Granted, I've said that line myself many, many times in the past, but for some reason over the last few years I get a physical reaction every time I hear it.

Here's my response to "It's easier said than done": NO SHIT. That is the most obvious statement that has ever come out of my mouth and I vow to you and Jesus that I will never say it to anyone again. Even worse, that statement always seems to follow a piece of wisdom or advice about life or healing or moving forward.

So, before we go any further: **LIFE IS HARD. HEALING HURTS. MOVING FORWARD IS SCARY FOR MOST PEOPLE.**

You can talk and talk and talk about what you want to do with your life. You can complain about anything and everything—but when it comes to real-life changes . . . well, that's easier said than done. Instead, people sit and talk and blow smoke out their asses and complain that they're not happy because of so-and-so and their circumstances. And to change or work on themselves is easier said than done. So they don't.

Well, I for one call bullshit. No more cop-outs. *Everything* is easier said than done. Words are meaningless unless they are backed up with action. *Everyone* knows that. I know one thing to be true: A fulfilled, happy, amazing, kick-ass life takes *work*. Work on yourself, work on your past, work on your issues, work on your addictions. If it were easy, in my humble opinion, there would be way less wrong with the world than there is now.

Yes, it's hard. But there is so much help out there—books, therapists, coaches, support groups. Help online and offline. There is not one single person I know who has an amazing life who hasn't found help, then taken hard action and worked on themselves. A LOT. And none of them will tell you that it was easy, nor did it look like a tampon commercial.

But you can do it. Start with this book. Wherever you are in your life . . . whether you have a heartbreaking story exactly like mine, or your own version . . . I wrote this book for you. I wrote it for all the women out there who are sick and tired of being sick and tired. Who are ready to take the bull by the horns and get shit done. Who are ready to play a bigger game. Yes, living a kick-ass life takes work, but I know how you can get there. Follow the advice in this book, examine yourself honestly, grab the bull by the horns, and go get that amazing life.

You are the most precious thing you've got. You are priceless and worth all the work in the world to make you happy and fulfilled. This life you have is short. You have such an immense amount of loving power within you. All you need is an ounce of belief that you can create what you want. Look for that crack in the door and run for it.

Live, love, and learn on your terms.

Hugs and ass kicking,

Andrea

CHAPTER 1

TAKE RESPONSIBILITY
for Your Life and Your Choices

In order for you to start your journey to a kick-ass existence, *you must take responsibility for your life.*

If you are someone who points fingers and blames everyone else for your unhappy circumstances, or feel that you are just "destined to have a crappy life," I'm talking to you.

If you are often the guest of honor at your own pity party and play the victim role too often, I'm talking to you.

If you're this person, you might be thinking, "Doesn't she know how hard I have it? Doesn't she know all the awful things that have happened to me?"

Here's the truth: Everyone has a sad story. Even heartbreaking ones. You're not unique that way. Neither am I, nor is your Jane Doe neighbor or any celebrity you see on the E! channel. The hard truth is that the longer you stay stuck in a story of blaming your circumstances, the more you keep repeating that story to yourself and to others, the more you will remain in this same story. Do you *want* to remain stuck? Do you *want* to remain in the same story? Then stop telling it from a place of victimhood.

Your circumstances don't mean you are "destined" for unhappiness. They don't mean anything except they are facts and life experiences. Bottom line: Your life is made up of your **circumstances**. How you react and **think** about them is what determines your **feelings** and **beliefs** about yourself, and what shapes your reality.

For example: Let's say you've gained twenty pounds in the last year from overeating and not exercising. Now you want to lose that weight.

The **circumstance** is that you're twenty pounds heavier than you want to be.

The **thought** you might have is that you're fat, lazy, and unattractive.

Your **belief** might be that you're never going to have a relationship that you want, or get that promotion, all because of the weight.

You might be **feeling** sadness, low self-esteem, or unworthiness. And when you're feeling this way, what do you think your actions might be? When people feel sad and unworthy, do you think they are motivated to maintain a healthy lifestyle and exercise? Probably not.

The thing with this pattern of thinking and subsequent feeling is that the actions taken are usually direct evidence of the original thought. So you might overeat, not exercise, and have a whirlwind of self-defeating and negative thoughts that make you feel even worse. Then your thought that, "I'm fat and unattractive" is supported by your actions. It becomes a cycle that can be hard to escape from when you're caught in it.

But again, it's not your circumstances that are making you feel a certain way—it's your thoughts about them. And believe it or not, you're *choosing* to keep those thoughts in your life.

Life is full of choices—big and small, conscious and subconscious. Some decisions scream at you (Should I take this job? Should I leave him?). Others are more subtle, like choosing your thoughts. I fully believe that you, with practice, can shift your thinking and choose your thoughts. You can let go of limited beliefs and self-critical insults, and then choose better ones.

What you want to do is turn negative **thoughts** into positive ones, which turn into committed **beliefs**. Those beliefs then create good **feelings**. And a person with good feelings, committed beliefs, and positive thoughts is likely to make smart choices that can lead to better **circumstances** and a kick-ass life.

I'm not asking you to move mountains here. Don't overachieve or even over-affirm. To turn around your thoughts, simply notice your negative thoughts, and force yourself to change them into something positive. Look at what an amazing impact this can have:

	NEGATIVE CHOICES	POSITIVE CHOICES
Circumstance	You're 20 pounds overweight.	You're 20 pounds overweight.
Thought	I'm fat, lazy, and unattractive.	I would love to lose weight by eating better and exercising.
Belief	I'm never going to have a good relationship, job, etc., because I'm too fat.	Eating healthier and exercising will give me more energy. I deserve to feel better.
Feeling	Sadness, low self-esteem, or unworthiness	Motivation, pride, self-worth
Outcome	Your weight stays the same.	You lose some weight and feel better.

See how changing your thoughts from negative to positive can create a drastically different outcome? It's not necessarily difficult to be committed to a thought or belief. Some of us feel so committed that we fill out a marriage license and get hitched. We can't see another way and really have never even looked. Now, that's commitment, wouldn't you say? If it seems like being committed to a positive choice is difficult, remind yourself of a negative choice you've committed to. See? You *can* commit.

Another example: Take a belief you have that you think is a fact. Not a circumstance (such as being in debt), but a belief. For example, "I can never get out of this debt." Ask yourself, "What if it was different?" You don't have to completely say the opposite to yourself, or repeat any far-reaching affirmation—just *get curious* about the idea that it could be different. What if it was possible to get out of debt? Just consider it. Try that with any belief you have that doesn't make you feel good. Or that isn't empowering. Beliefs like, "All the good guys are either gay or taken." Or, "I'm too fat to go to the gym."

What if they were different?

And here's another perspective. Often women become committed to disempowering beliefs because we've made a big deal about something we didn't need to. We created drama (I'm sure *you've* never done that, right?) around something in our minds, and before we know it we're in a panic or planning our own funeral.

One of my favorite all-time questions in those situations is, "What if it just wasn't a big deal?" Allow yourself to back the hell up and really determine if your belief is really that big a deal.

Most of the time it's not. Own your life as it *really* is now. When you start taking responsibility for your life—your circumstances, your thoughts, your feelings, your beliefs—you can change it for the better. You can make smarter choices that lead to results that make you happy.

One of the best pieces of advice my dad gave me: You don't *have* to do anything; that's a choice, too. Just know there are consequences in your choices. And dad was 100 percent right.

CHAPTER 2

CANNONBALL OUT
of Your Comfort Zone

Comfort zones, to many people, are like crack to crackheads. They get addicted to their comfort zone. They don't want to be away from it. When pulled away from their comfort zone, they break out into a sweat, throw fits, and just plain freak the hell out.

There's nothing wrong with wanting to be safe in your life (as for crack, that's a different story). As human beings, we are wired to want and need safety. Safety can look like seat belts; like looking for cars before you cross the street; like avoiding zombies; like not eating raw meat—stuff like that. But the real magic in building your *biggest, most kick-ass life* happens *outside* of your comfort zone.

Think about it. Attaining anything in your life that has made you really happy and fulfilled has probably made you a little uncomfortable.

You've had to stretch your limits, go against limiting beliefs, and endure a little (or a lot) of fear. Whether it was running for student body president, asking for a date, or applying for a job, all of those things require a bit of a stretch.

You might look at other people and think they have had it easier than you. News flash: They didn't. I don't believe for one hot second that anyone you admire has had smooth sailing when it comes to his or her decisions and actions. They've been scared. They've had that nauseating gut feeling. They've had those dramatic, tear-filled phone conversations with their besties. It happens to everyone.

Answer these questions:

- What is something you want to do that is out of your comfort zone?
- What is the real reason you haven't done it, if it's really something you want?

I'm going to assume it's because of that four-letter "f word": FEAR. Let's look at some of the different types of fear that stepping out of your comfort zone can elicit:

- Fear of failure
- Fear of success
- Fear of judgment/criticism from others
- Fear of commitment

The list could go on and on. And if I had to guess, you have all of these fears.

I hate to break it to you, but you're not the only one who has a list of fears about going after what you want. Maybe you can find some comfort in the fact that we *all* do. The only difference between those people who go after their dreams and step out of their comfort zone, and those who don't, is . . . action. Flipping fear the finger and finding the courage and confidence either while you're doing it or even afterwards.

It's true.

So I invite you to air out your fear story. What are you afraid might happen? I want the whole enchilada story. Drama and all. Go ahead.

Now that you've gotten it all out, I lovingly ask you . . .

Do you *really* think this will happen? Could this really be a true story? And even if in some crazy alternate Universe where fear stories actually come true, would it kill you?

For example: I had a client who wanted to quit her job to start her own business. She hated her job and was in love with what she really wanted to do. Months after declaring to the Universe that she really wanted to change, she was offered an early retirement with a five-month severance package. Or she could stay at her job. Awesome opportunity, right?

But she was afraid she would run out of money; that her new business would fail; that she would look stupid and foolish. It was all just too scary and too far out of her comfort zone.

So I asked her: What if you run out of money? Can you get another part-time job?

Her answer: Yes.

Me: Do you really feel in your heart that this business will fail?

Her answer: No.

Me: And even if by some unforeseen chance that it does, would the world stop turning? Could you just start over?

Her answer: Yes.

Once she was able to look her fears in the eye and question them, the catastrophic stories took the shape of what they really were: bullshit. I'm happy to report that she gleefully took the package, left her job, and started her own dream business. Was she scared shitless? Yes. But she did it anyway.

So when you consider your fears of going outside your comfort zone, ask yourself: Are you going to regret not doing this? I ask my clients this all the time: In one year from now, will you wish you had started right now? Or when you're eighty, are you going to regret not doing it? Seriously . . .

On your deathbed, are you going to be okay with the fact that you didn't step out of your comfort zone and do the thing your heart so desperately wanted you to do?

If you answered, "Yes, I'll be totally fine and content not following my heart," I have to ask . . . why are you reading this book?!

My "thing" was roller derby. I remember seeing those ladies on TV when I was a little girl back in the '70s, thinking they were the toughest, coolest, rowdiest ladies ever. And now I'm almost forty years old and roller derby has made a comeback. My inner critic says I'm too old. I'll get hurt and probably look stupid. But you know what? I did it anyway. Was I scared? Yes. Did I gather all the courage I could before I went? Nope. I just went and figured out the courage later.

Because never in a million years did I want to tell my children and grandchildren this story of how awesome and badass I think it would have been to do it, and follow it up with, "But, I was too old, so I didn't do it."

That's a lame-ass story.

Truth be told, I wanted to do it for about seven years before I finally decided it was time. I was too scared, too busy, too pregnant (well, that's actually a valid excuse not to play roller derby), too whatever for seven long years.

And besides, isn't it way more awesome to be the one who isn't the "ideal person" for whatever your big thing is and to go out and do it anyway? To be the seventy-five-year-old woman running a marathon for the first time? Or the person with no photography or business background starting his or her own photography business? Aren't they the most badass people anyway? The underdogs, the unexpected?

Stepping out of your comfort zone doesn't mean doing something major and crazy. Some people love jumping out of airplanes. Those aren't necessarily the types of things I'm talking about.

What if you painted your room the color you love? Or completely changed your hair to a new style you've been eyeing? Or join a co-ed softball team, or a quilting club, or take up again a hobby that you let go of a long time ago because "life" got in the way.

There will always be excuses. There will always be fear stories. We are all masters at coming up with them. Hell, we should be able to add that skill to our resumes by now. It's up to you to call yourself out on your own bullshit and move your butt.

What would it take for you to do this? Letting go of your dramatic fear story for just five minutes, maybe? Start there. And see what happens.

The thing is, many times the excuses come up because the things out of our comfort zone seem so scary and big. And they very well might be. But if you look at the whole mountain, you'll always be scared and maybe try to get out of climbing it.

Instead, just look at the first step. The first step might be doing a simple Google search to research something. Or telling someone about it (see Chapter 5 for more on that). The point is that doing little things out of your comfort zone helps you gain momentum. You have no excuse *not* to start doing little things. The best part about little things is that they lead to bigger and bigger things. Pretty soon, you're farther up the mountain than you ever thought you could get.

CHAPTER 3

Ask Your Friends How You Can SUPPORT THEM

Why would I dedicate an entire chapter to being of service to others? Because helping out your friends (or even strangers) is the fastest and easiest way to forget your own problems. Being of service to others is never about you. (If you make it about you, you might want to think about why people don't want you to help them. Just a thought.) And I figured that if you picked up this book, chances are you have problems every once in a while like the rest of us mortals.

If you think about the fact that people are biologically wired for human connection, but still try to solve problems and heal all by themselves, doesn't that sound a little backwards? Many times, we don't know people are suffering until they are *really, really* in pain. When it's an absolute *emergency*. And it just plain sucks. I believe it truly takes a village to create a kick-ass life.

Let's say you're feeling stuck in a quicksand-like drama-o-rama of your own. You've been thinking (or maybe obsessing) about a problem in your life and you've gone down the rabbit hole of trying to fix it. Maybe you feel sorry for yourself about this problem or maybe you just generally feel like crap about it. When this happens, try this: Reach out to someone else. Even if you think she doesn't need help. No need to make assumptions or accusations about her potential problems, just ask in a really open way.

The conversation can look like this:

YOU: Hey, friend. What's going on?

YOUR FRIEND: Well, nothing much. Same 'ol, same 'ol.

YOU: Is there anything you need support with? How can I support you?

YOUR FRIEND: Whaaaaaat?

YOU: I know, it sounds weird. But I just want you to know if there's anything going on in your life that you need support around, I'm here to listen or help you in any way I can. So, what's going on?

Your friend may be slightly taken aback, slightly suspicious, hang up on you because she thinks she's being *Punk'd*, who knows. The point is, many times we get into our routines with our friends, take them for granted, and forget how important it is to help. You never know unless you ask. And there's a good possibility you have a friend with a situation she's dealing with right now. That one is easy-peasy because you already have something specific to ask her about.

Another tip: Sometimes it's okay to just be honest. For example: You might get that friend who says, "Oh, I don't want to talk about me. What's going on with you?" And you can respond honestly by telling her that you're tired of going around and around about *your* shit and that you're wanting to get your mind off it by helping her. That way it's all out there on the table.

One of the side effects of being of service is feeling good about yourself. I think our culture tells us that being of service should solely be altruistic and that feeling good while doing it is negative and selfish. I vehemently disagree. It's okay and, in my opinion, even awesome to feel good about yourself while being of service. The only thing to be careful about is if your service is conditional on external feedback. In other words, if you're attached to the outcome to bring you good feelings and don't otherwise feel good about yourself, you need to first do some inner work on *you* so you're not relying on your service actions to bring you what you need.

Keep in mind that being of service means that you don't expect anything in return. That includes a thank you (that's a favor). So try to remain unattached to the outcome when you decide to be of service to others. Sometimes it's a thankless job (if you're a parent, you'll understand this), but don't let that stop you.

And please, please don't do it if your reason for doing it is to make you look good in front of others. You're better off just not doing it at all. The true definition of service is to help; an act of helpful activity; aid. Nowhere in that definition is "helping peeps so you can look awesome."

You'll also find that the more you open yourself up to support others, the more you'll start to get it back. Being open to accepting that support is actually a gift to that person wanting to help you. So take it if you're offered some!

CHAPTER 4

Uncover Your
PERSONAL VALUES

Your unique, personal values are so important to your overall happiness. I'm not talking about your "valuables." These aren't grandma's 100-year-old china dolls. I'm talking about your *values*.

Let me ask you one simple question: What's important to you? Many of us know what our family's values were when we grew up. Or you know what the values of your religion are. Or your culture.

But what are *yours*?

(For the sake of this chapter and the importance of this topic, I'm giving you permission to flip the bird to all of those values that were put upon you if they aren't really yours. Or to anyone who tells you what "should" be important to you.)

Your values are the things that are important to *you*. Most people have never taken the time to list out their personal values. They may indeed still be the same as your parents' values, your religion, or your culture. But there are probably more that you haven't yet fully recognized.

To compile a full list of your values, start by answering these questions: What is important about the way you live your life? For example, is it important that you connect with others on a deep level consistently? Or do you have a need to be responsible to our planet? Are you passionate about parenting a certain way and want to educate others about it?

These specific things are rooted into your values.

Another way to tap into your values is to think about what really pisses you off. Chances are, when something makes you angry, underneath is a value that is being stepped on.

To help you get started, here is a short list of common values:

ABUNDANCE	HAPPINESS
BOLDNESS	HONESTY
COMMUNITY	HUMOR
EDUCATION	INTEGRITY
FAMILY	INTIMACY
FREEDOM	KINDNESS
FUN	MAKING A DIFFERENCE
GRATITUDE	SPIRITUALITY

There are many, many more. (Do a quick Google search to find more values that might resonate with you.) Another tip is to define key values or string several together to really nail down what it is that's important to you. For instance, what the value *freedom* looks like to you might look different to the next person. Freedom to you might look like free-spiritedness, but to someone else perhaps it's independence. Be open to describing exactly what it is.

When you're making this list, try to stay away from tangible things (we'll get to those in Chapter 13). If you keep coming back to gourmet food and you think that's your value, think about what gourmet food actually brings you. Is it the creativity that cooking offers that you really crave? Or connecting with friends while cooking or eating? It's not actually the *thing,* but the feeling it brings you.

Once you have your list, don't stop there. The next step is to ask yourself how alive these values are in your life. Rate (on a scale of one to ten with ten being the highest) how well each value is being honored in your life right now. For example, say you have physical wellness/fitness on your list of values, but for whatever reason you haven't exercised in a few months. Or a few years. So obviously, that value would score low even though it is something that's important to you. Give it a two.

A lot of times, we aren't fully honoring *all* of our values at the same time. Things tend to fall by the wayside—which is normal—but if you have a go-to list of what's important to you, it's easier to see that, *yes*, values are important, and *no*, it's not selfish for you to make time for these things in your life.

Here's something that's really important about your values: They are yours. They are not up for judgment or ridicule from others. Ever. **If it's important to you, it should be important to you, period.**

The next step in this assignment is for you to look at the values you scored low on. Think of one or two things you can do immediately to raise the rating. If fitness scored low and it's one of your values, commit to something simple like taking a walk this week.

I am a firm believer that your personal values are just as important to you as your basic needs such as food, water, and shelter. Sure, you won't physically *die* if they aren't being honored in your life, but in a way, your spirit dies a little when they aren't. For instance, let's say your top three values are honesty, spirituality, and creativity—they scored eight, nine, and ten, respectively. And say you work in a job where the company is doing something illegal and they're asking you to cover for them. If you say no, you risk losing your job. And on top of that, your job is so demanding that you haven't had time to tap into any spirituality that makes you feel good, nor had any time to fuel your creative needs.

How do you think your day-to-day life would be? Shitty, right?

Your excuse might be that the job is just temporary. And you'll find the time later for spirituality and creativity.

But you have the power to determine what is acceptable and unacceptable in your life. You are creating your awful feelings by tolerating your own decisions.

By having a list of your own values, you're creating a blueprint for what makes you happy, brings you joy and fulfillment, and at the same time shows you what is making you unhappy. If you find a lot of values that score one, two, or three on your list, make time to focus on them, a little bit at a time. Make no mistake—if you really commit to doing these exercises, it will undoubtedly lead to positive changes in your life. Living your life more in line with your values will help you find that happier, healthier you.

CHAPTER 5

Tell Five People about
YOUR SECRET DREAM

I believe we're all dreamers, even if you don't feel like one. Dreamers fall into two categories:

1. The action takers—whether you research all angles and possibilities before taking action or just start quickly, throwing caution to the wind.
2. Those who dream and do nothing about it.

Here's the thing about dreams: we often convince ourselves it's "just a dream." We keep it a secret in the back pocket of our hearts, or maybe confide in one person. Plans of action are rarely discussed. It goes nowhere, so our belief that "it's just a dream" is confirmed.

I don't know about you, but that, to me, is a bunch of shit.

This chapter is for those of you who keep your dreams to yourselves out of fear:

- Fear of the reaction of others.
- Fear of not being supported, or even fear of being supported.
- Fear of what might happen if you tell someone about your dream and then you change your mind.
- Fear of trying and failing.
- Fear of actually *doing* something about your dream.

Most, if not all, red-blooded human beings have a dream. It may be small; it may be big and grandiose. Could be moving out of your hometown; could be world domination. It may be the same dream you've had since you were a kid, or your dream may change every month. There is no right or wrong way to dream. Just like your values, your dreams are yours. They are not up for ridicule or judgment from you or anyone else.

I've got some questions for you . . .

- What is your secret dream?
- What is important to you about it?
- On a scale from 1–10, how excited are you about it?
- Now, what are you going to do about it?

(I just lit a fire under you, didn't I?)

Here's a challenge for you: Tell five people about your secret dream. It's important that those five people don't stomp on your dream. (If they do, remember this: their negative crap about *your* dream has nothing to do with you or your dream. It's 100 percent about their inability to have enough balls to even for one second think their dream can come true. It's about *their* insecurities and fears; mixed in with some envy that you have the balls to articulate your dream.)

Enough about balls.

The thing about telling people about your big dream is that when you do, it becomes real. No, not like waving a magic wand and *poof! it's here*, but saying it out loud gives it power. You're committing to yourself, to another person, and to the Universe. You're actually putting energy out there that creates *feelings* inside of you. And P.S. when you do tell someone about it, check how your body feels. Are you tingly? Did you feel a flip-flop in your stomach? If it scares the shit out of you, you're really onto something. If you felt excited, that's very telling. In fact, it's your crystal ball answer to the question of "Should I do this?"

A couple more interesting things might happen when you talk about it.

1. The person you told might tell you theirs and you can excitedly giggle with each other about your secret dreams. Or, not as fun and sexy . . .

2. Your inner critic might interrupt and tell you why you can't fulfill this dream (see Chapter 21 for more on this). Or the other person's inner critic interrupts and tells you why you can't or shouldn't fulfill this dream.

If #2 happens (pun intended), this does not mean your dream sharing is over and it can go back to just living in your head. No, ma'am. It just means that you're on to something really, really big. And I mean really big.

Because that's the thing with inner critics. They get *real* pissed when you're onto something big and exciting. So now you can use that as an indicator instead of a dream squasher. Think of it as your own internal barometer. When thinking about a dream and you get ridiculously scared, let that be your giant, green, flashing light saying THIS IS IT.

Another thing about sharing your dreams: You assume accountability. It's similar to working with a life coach—you share your dreams, work through your fears, commit to action, and your coach holds you accountable. There's no, "Sure, I'm really going to do this!" and then no one asks you about it again so you're off the hook. Nope.

So when you tell your five people, tell them you'd like some accountability. Ask them to ask you about it again in a week, or a month.

Let me say one more thing about creating witnesses to your dreams and then taking action on it: In the grand scheme of this life, we're all here for only a microsecond. Whether your last day is today or any day . . . at the end of your life how do you want to describe how it was?

Awesome?

Peaceful?

Kick-ass?

Fulfilling?

You get to choose.

Your dreams are your dreams. And if you keep them to yourself, you're less likely to see them materialize. And in my humble opinion, that is one of the saddest things in the whole wide world.

CHAPTER 6

LISTEN TO YOUR GUT
(Not Just the Stuff You Want to Hear)

Your gut. Your intuition. Your spirit. Your soul's compass. God. The Universe. Higher Power. Call it what you want, but the fact of the matter is that you have one: a voice inside you that is your guiding compass.

Most people get to know their intuition when they've heard it, but pushed it aside like cold green beans they didn't want to eat. Lo and behold, the situation didn't turn out the way they wanted it to, or let's be honest—things just completely fell apart. Could be a relationship, or making a purchase, or taking a job.

(Because lord knows, we've all had that feeling or voice that said, *"Hmm. Not really sure about this person. Kind of an asshole."* But we date them anyway. And sometimes marry them. How's that working out, hmmm?)

On the other hand, sometimes you'll have a great idea or thought, but then that voice pops up in the form of pesky logic and reasoning, and you change your mind. Then later, you find out your first reaction or your idea was the correct one.

For instance, think about a specific time when your intuition spoke loud and clear to you. Maybe it was about a person, a new job, or a new opportunity. Did you listen?

And tell me, my friend, if you didn't listen, what ended up happening?

If you ignored your (correct) intuition, don't beat yourself up. Most people's first experience with actually realizing their intuition has spoken to them was when they *didn't* listen to it. Case in point: Right after my divorce I dated a guy who turned out to be a complete nightmare. And I'm not exaggerating at all. I remember on our first date thinking, "Something isn't right, but I don't know what." But he was tall and handsome, charming, and funny as hell and I thought he was Mr. Right. On our second date my gut was telling me much louder to *run*. I still can't tell you what exactly it was that made me feel that way. It wasn't anything glaringly obvious. But I felt it, ignored it, and nine months later the whole thing blew up in my face.

Intuition isn't complex. It's not rocket science. It shouldn't take a lot of thinking, energy, magic beans, or any other special powers. It just needs to be listened to. Here's what intuition might look like:

- Listening to your "aha" feelings even if they make no sense and don't fit the picture of how you think things should be.
- Paying attention to your body's signals and then staying away from people who suck the energy from you.
- Listening to the good kind of "goosebumps" as a sign to say *Hell yes* when you're making a decision about something.
- Taking action on what moves and inspires you rather than only making decisions based on what seems logical on paper.

If you feel like you need help here, there are ways to strengthen not only your intuition itself but also your ability to listen to it. (Let me preface this by saying this work may feel and sound a bit "woo-woo" and for stoned hippies, but it will help you find clarity. Woo-woo or not, just keep an open mind and get to work.)

First, practice asking your intuition questions. Ask out loud, or write your questions down. Ask yourself whatever it is that you want to know. Questions might be:

- What do I know to be true here?
- Is this a *Hell yes* for me?
- What does my heart truly want here?

Then, get quiet, wait, and listen. Because your intuition can only help you if you're listening. Your intuition's answer is usually the first thing that comes to you. Keep this in mind: It may not be what you want to hear. We tend to screen these intuitional messages and only want to act on the ones that are easy, won't hurt us or anyone else, and have a guaranteed outcome.

Last time I checked, life didn't work that way.

Also, check in with your body here. If you feel heaviness or darkness, chances are that is your intuition telling you the answer is no.

Like a lot of people, you might find that intuitional messages evoke feelings of fear. As a result, I get this question a lot: *How do I distinguish what is fear and what is my intuition? Sometimes I confuse that "gut feeling."* Great question!

Here are some tips to help decipher the two:

1. Fear lives in your head, and intuition is in your heart and body. Generally speaking, fear is much louder and intrusive. Intuition tends to speak to you in more of a whisper that is inexplicable and is unattached to the outcome of your decision, whereas fear is insistent and based on its perceived logic.

2. Fear is a darker emotion that will present itself through physical reactions to thoughts (examples: sweating, feeling an adrenaline rush, and just generally freaking out). Intuition is a lighter feeling that, if listened to, should not evoke panic. Fear can make you want to get the hell out of dodge, hide, and avoid what you think is coming, whereas intuition is about understanding the possible dangers but having the faith and trust in yourself to move forward.

3. Fear lives in the land of worst possible scenario and intuition lives in the present. When you find yourself thinking of that crazy-ass fear story from Chapter 2, *that* will be your indication that you're dealing with fear, not intuition.

BOTTOM LINE: Your intuition is rooting for you. It's your biggest cheerleader, your biggest fan. Your watchdog and bodyguard. It has your back at all times. It lives in your body and speaks to you. Think of it as the fiercest and sweetest pit bull you've ever met, in the form of an angel.

There is absolutely nothing else like it. And it never gives up on you.

You just have to listen to it.

CHAPTER 7

STOP APOLOGIZING
and People Pleasing

I included both in this chapter because I've found that people pleasers tend to be chronic apologizers and vice versa. They go together like pork and beans.

I'll start with people pleasers. People pleasers are everywhere. And it's no wonder—we all want people to like us, to be accepted, and to be loved. So we run around nutty as a fruitcake saying yes to everyone as if our lives depended on it.

But of course, there is hope.

Here are some suggestions to help you stop people pleasing. Keep in mind, they all take practice. Find the ones that work for you and keep practicing them until they get easier. Change won't come overnight, but it will come. The key is to make sure you're pleasing yourself before anyone else.

- **Remember, you make your own decisions.** I'll repeat this in several chapters until you are sick of hearing it because it's true of everything. It's one of those things that you'll need to remind yourself over and over again. Even some of the most evolved people I know *still* are practicing the power of taking responsibility for their choices. You have a choice, even when you're saying yes when you don't want to. Don't forget it. (See Chapter 1 if you need a refresher on owning your choices.)

- **Buy yourself some time.** When asked to do something, chances are you don't *have* to give an answer right then and there. If you're still practicing saying no and it feels very uncomfortable for you, you can say, "Let me check my calendar." Or, "Lemme ask my Magic 8 Ball," or "I'll have to check with my husband and then I'll get back to you tomorrow." Any one of those will work. The extra time might help you find some strength to say no.

- **Try the "If it's not a 'Hell yes,' it's a 'Hell no'" mantra.** This mantra was given to me by one of my own mentors, Jeanna Gabelinni, and has quite literally changed my life. When asked to do something, ask yourself if it's a "Hell yes." You'll probably know immediately. If it's not, even if it's a "Hell maybe," it's a "Hell no." Using this mantra also might help you become more aware of how often you're saying yes when you don't want to, just for the sake of people pleasing.

- **Create a go-to routine before you give an answer.** A few years ago, I was listening to a podcast by Brené Brown. She said when asked to do something, she spins her wedding ring on her finger in three complete circles before she gives an answer. (The example she used was when she was asked to make three dozen cupcakes for her daughter's class the next morning. She spun her ring . . . and politely said no.) Like with asking for extra time to make an answer, this quick routine will give you time to take a breath, ask yourself the hell no/hell yes question, and respond accordingly.

- **Don't pile on the excuses.** This tends to happen because you're uncomfortable saying no and want to fill the awkward space, even though you're probably imagining that awkward space in the first place. If you find yourself making excuse after excuse, just stop, notice, and don't give any more.

- **When you say no, tell yourself what you're actually saying yes to.** There's always something—more time with your kids, time to go to the gym, a less stressful week. If you can't think of anything tangible, know what you're always saying yes to is yourself.
- **Avoid making up a fear story of what the outcome will be if you say no.** Oftentimes, people imagine these catastrophic fallouts of what will happen if they don't say yes to the request. Someone will be mad at us or hate us. You'll lose your job. You'll rot in hell. Watch your thoughts here and ask yourself if that story is really true. Chances are, it's one of those crazy fear stories from Chapter 2 that's never going to come true.

All of this brings me to apologizing. Chronic apologizing can be an all-out life sucker. Many women I know apologize for who they are by following up their opinion with, "I'm sorry, but that's just who I am." I myself used to say that statement often when I was speaking my truth and knew people weren't going to like it. Many women apologize for what they believe in, for their dreams and ambitions, for anything where other people don't agree with them. When you're apologizing in that way, it comes from fear, not from your heart. Think of it this way. There are two types of apologies:

1. The first comes from your heart, when you are truly remorseful for something you have done or said and are seeking forgiveness from that other person. You're taking responsibility for yourself, and that is an act of love, an act of empowerment.

2. The second is an act of fear: fear of making someone else mad, of someone not liking you, or fear of not pleasing someone. By doing this, you're simply disempowering yourself.

Chronic, fear-based apologizing can run pretty deep. It can be a sign that you don't feel like you're enough. It can say a lot about your self-esteem and self-confidence. Even more sadly, by apologizing chronically, you can end up creating more low self-esteem and it becomes a chicken-or-egg situation.

If this sounds like you, try these tips to get off the apology train:

- Be aware. It starts there, sister. Try to keep track and notice whenever you say "Sorry." Is it in your normal conversation as often as the word "the"?
- When you find yourself about to say "Sorry," stop yourself before the word comes out of your mouth and ask yourself if you are truly feeling remorseful at that moment or if it's something else. Are you instead feeling embarrassed, confused, guilty, frustrated, or maybe needing to feel validated about something from the other person? Can you pinpoint what you're really feeling instead? If so, deal with that emotion; don't apologize.
- Dovetailing off the last point, if you're not ready to express the way you're really feeling, try to have a mantra that you either say to yourself or say out loud. What if instead of saying, "I'm sorry," you said, "I'm . . . amazing!" or "I'm . . . absolutely fantastic right at this moment." Yes, people might look at you like you're nuts, but it's good practice.

If you work on these two things, I promise you'll get to a place where you feel more like the real you. Your most authentic self doesn't need to people please or apologize profusely. Start strengthening this muscle and you'll see an about-face in the way you feel about yourself.

CHAPTER 8

Bad Relationships Are
GREAT LIFE LESSONS

If you've been cheated on, disrespected, or verbally or physically abused, join the club. There are *millions* of us (hence dedicating an entire chapter to it). No matter what the problem was in your bad relationship, it's possible to move on, move forward, learn a ton, and be a much better, kick-ass person and partner for your next relationship. I was cheated on in my first marriage (I'll call him "Cheater A"). Soon after we divorced, I started dating. Why so soon? Basically, I was heartbroken, vulnerable, and yes, a little desperate.

At first I met some nice, normal guys. But I didn't want anything to do with them. I managed to find a guy who mirrored what I was: heartbroken, vulnerable, and desperate (I'll call him "Cheater B"). We were quite a pair. A few months into the relationship, he cheated on me. I remember crumbling in a heap on my bedroom floor the moment I found out. My head was spinning and I kept repeating, "I can't believe this is happening again. I can't believe this is happening again . . ."

After the second time in a row being cheated on, I knew something was wrong with what *I* was doing. Yes, being cheated on is the ultimate betrayal. But when it happened to me twice in a row, I was forced to take a long, hard look at myself, what I was choosing, what I was putting up with, and what I learned.

If you've ever been there or somewhere like it, yes, it sucks ass. However, whether you're out of the relationship, or still in it, sitting down and reflecting on what you learned can be immensely helpful to you and your self-growth. Here are some of the goodies I learned:

- **If you've been cheated on, it isn't about you.** It wasn't my fault the guys I was with screwed around. It's about them—their issues, insecurities, and reasons. People who cheat are never in a place of sound mind or of their highest, best self. Many times we ask, "How could you do this to me?" . . . but it's really not about us. Now, you can't blame the other person for your heartbreak long-term, but stop blaming yourself for the act itself.
- **Being broken up with doesn't mean you're not pretty enough, skinny enough, or good enough in bed.** I spent countless nights awake obsessing about what I could have done differently. What if I'd had bigger boobs? Is she prettier? Funnier? Etc., etc., and on and on until my head would explode. Here's the thing: *There is no definite answer here.* You'll go bananas trying to find it but you never will, because it's not about you. You are amazing just as you are.
- **Being broken up with didn't mean you're "bad" at relationships.** After Cheater B and I broke up, I was convinced I was the suckiest partner on earth. I vowed to be alone; I even considered joining the convent and becoming a nun. My self-analysis post Cheater B made me realize I was actually good at relationships (but could be even better), just not so good at picking the right partners. Which brings me to . . .

- **You need to think about why you're picking certain partners.** I had *chosen* to stay in a relationship and marry Cheater A even though I knew he wasn't right for me. I *chose* to jump into a new relationship with Cheater B when I knew deep down I needed to work on myself first. Sure, I didn't necessarily know they would cheat on me, but I knew they weren't right for me, either. Yes, I had picked them both, chosen to stay, and I had to take responsibility for that. I was such a mess after Cheater A that I 100 percent believe that Cheater B knew I was perfect for him: I was someone easy to manipulate, quick to "fall in love," and willing to stick through anything. "Like attracts like" and I attracted a shit-pile of a mess.

- **Breakups are something you need to grieve and get over as an event.** Think of the breakup separately from the relationship as well as the person you were in the relationship with. What I found was that being cheated on was fucking traumatic. Drama-filled. The suspicions, the lies, the fights, the moment of finding out. It was an *event*. I really had to come to terms with it and grieve it separately than the breakup of the relationship. In some small way, it still stings sometimes to think about it. That's okay. It doesn't mean anything. Just because it still hurts doesn't mean I miss the relationship or the Cheater. Just that it hurt, and sucked.

- **Frequent bad relationships might be an indicator that you don't know what it's like to be in a normal, functional, healthy relationship.** This one was shocking to me, and might be to you, too. When I met my current husband, I had to run back to my therapist. I told her I knew the relationship was great, but I was soooooo bored. She told me that my past relationships were so full of drama and intensity that now that I was in a normal, healthy relationship, I didn't know how to act. Talk about a wake-up call! I had to learn healthy communication (you mean we *don't* scream at each other and slam doors?), as well as the fact that healthy relationships are sometimes *quiet and uneventful.* Humph. Who knew?

- **Bad breakups might help you trust your intuition.** And this, my friends, was the "big shit" of lessons. I ignored my intuition *big time* in both my relationships with Cheaters A and B. There were times with Cheater B that my intuition was flashing red lights and sirens at me and I walked right by. I was in a place where I would rather be in a bad relationship than no relationship. I was so ashamed of where I was; I stayed with him so no one would know how bad it was. My intuition *never left me.* It tried and tried to help me and never gave up. Finally, I could not take one more day, so I left. Had I listened much earlier, I would have saved myself so much heartache. Practice the exercises in Chapter 6 to help you become an expert intuition truster.

I completely understand that when you're in that dark place of an unhealthy relationship—whether you're in it or it just ended— it's hard to see *any* good coming out of it and you may want to punch me in the face for telling you it will get better. But trust me when I tell you by doing the hard work and self-analysis you'll become a better person for having been through it. I learned so much from my bad relationships, and for that, I am eternally grateful. I don't regret one single day. For if I did, I would be regretting the person I am today.

CHAPTER 9

Find the Fastest
WAY TO PEACE

Part of living a kick-ass life is knowing how to make yourself happy. That's not easy for many women because we live in a cloud of self-doubt and confusion about what we really, really want. Making positive choices (see Chapter 1) that lead to happiness isn't always easy. Sometimes it's easier to hold on to negative feelings like anger, embarrassment, or sadness simply because we're used to it.

Here's an example. I sat in my therapist's office one evening, about a week or two after the fateful day my marriage fell apart. My soon-to-be ex-husband had been telling everyone who would listen, including his family, which had also been *my* family for the past thirteen years, lies about me. I was furious. Horrified. I wanted to choke him and kick him in the balls simultaneously. To say I saw red was an understatement.

I spewed in her office how much I hated him, how unfair it was that I could not defend myself to those people that I still loved. My name was being dragged through the mud and there was nothing I could do about it. I told her all the plans I had for clearing my name, which included e-mailing everyone I knew, to call a meeting and set things straight. If that didn't work, I would call them one by one to explain my side of the story. To me, all of this sounded completely reasonable and right.

She asked me what it was that I really wanted in all of this. I told her I wanted the truth to be told. That he was wrong for what he had done and said, and that I was right.

She said: "Sure, you can do all of these things. But . . .

Would you rather be right, or would you rather be free?"

I remember being stunned by what she said. Damn her and those "healthy" ways of being. She was right, though. I had to find the fastest, easiest way to peace.

For the first time I realized I had a choice to be free, a choice to be at peace. For the first time I realized I had the power when it came to my feelings and emotions. I realized that by acting on my impulsive wants, I would just create more negative feelings, drama, and chaos in my life. And I was tired. I was done.

So I let it go. I chose freedom and peace. It was one of the hardest things I've ever done, especially then, in the middle of all that turmoil. Creating the ultimate peace in this circumstance also meant I needed to forgive him.

Now, granted, I didn't forgive him that day, but the seed had been planted. For a while, there was part of me that wanted revenge. I wanted him to suffer. To pay for what he had done to me.

But the other part of me wanted freedom. Freedom from the pain I was putting myself through. Freedom from the uncertainty of our future. Freedom from who I was when I was with him. Freedom from the shackles I had created from holding on to any notion that things would ever be different.

Yes, it was a shitty circumstance. My marriage was over. I was alone for the first time. Ever. There was nothing I could do about that. Regardless of what your particular shitty circumstance is, you probably have some anger or sadness associated with it. And you probably want to act on that anger and sadness, just like I did. Ask yourself if those actions will truly free you from your negative feelings, or if they're likely to just create more of the same.

Hating my ex didn't change my circumstance. Explaining my side wouldn't turn back time so I could change events. Resenting him and the situation did nothing but keep me miserable. Hell, for all I knew, he didn't give a shit if I was happy or miserable, so if *I had to choose* . . .

Bingo. *I had to choose.*

And I chose peace.

It took many months for me to forgive him. I didn't need him to ask me for forgiveness, I just did it. I sat in the car one day at a stoplight near where he worked and I said out loud to myself, "I'm done hating you. You're forgiven."

It was easier than I thought. Yes, there were still times when I slipped back and would feel bitterness rise up in me when I would think of him and what happened, but I would simply remind myself that I no longer wished to hold onto those feelings.

When you find yourself in your own battle, or what feels like a fight, ask yourself what you can do to find peace for yourself. For example, if you're agonizing over a decision, ask yourself: *What would make this easier? What can I let go of for this to be not so hard?* Many times it's something right under our noses, but we are so stuck letting our egos run the show, we can't see any other way.

Remember, we can't control other people's *anything* (see Chapter 23), so even if it means letting go of a fight, letting go of money, letting go of "winning," do it. If you have peace and ease in your life, you are always winning, you are always rich, and you are always right with *you.*

CHAPTER 10

GET OVER Your Ex

The first time I got dumped I was fourteen. He was my first boyfriend and after about six months of dating, he walked me to class, handed me a note, and that was it. Tears streamed down my face in math class as I read, "I feel like we're just friends who hold hands." In other words, Mr. First Boyfriend dumped me because I wouldn't go to second base with him.

The second time, I was sixteen and we had been dating a whole year. He dumped me to "spend more time with his friends," which I found out really meant he wanted to date a cute freshman who had been flirting with him.

Then when I was thirty, my husband dumped me. So, it's fair to say that, like most of us, I've had some experience in this department.

Over the last few years, I've received many e-mails from women all over the world, pouring out their hearts about some guy who dumped them. They tell me everything they did for this guy, that they are so brokenhearted, and they end the e-mail with "Please help me. What should I do?"

While every situation is unique, I've compiled a list of things that, in retrospect, I've learned. I've made some mistakes in my journey to healing that have dragged out the process. But here are the most important things I've learned along the way, in hopes that they can help you avoid my mistakes.

Quit Stalking Him

Don't just unfriend him on Facebook, block him. Don't Google him, don't drive by his house, don't send him innocent "hi" texts, don't tell your friend to tell him you've been thinking about him, nothing. No stalking, no following, no "checking in." Don't pretend you're friends with him. After all, what do we usually do with friends? Confide, talk about who we're dating now—do you really want to do that with your ex? Do you want to hear about which girls he thinks are hot on Match.com? If you can truthfully say you have absolutely no emotional attachment to him at all, and it doesn't hurt one bit, knock yourself out. But I'm guessing that's not the case.

Yes, it will be so hard to avoid him completely. And you may slip, but try harder next time. Think about this: Do you feel *good* when you do any of this behavior? Do you think any of this is helping you heal, or helping him want to be with you, or helping *anything*? Truth: The only thing you're getting out of this is feeling worse about yourself and your situation. Is that what you want? Remember, it's your choice.

Give Yourself Enough Time to Grieve

When my ex-husband dumped me, and after the fog had cleared, I picked myself up and looked for the fast track to heal. I went to therapy, read self-help books, joined support groups—all the things I was supposed to do during a divorce. When people said, "The only thing that will heal you is time," I wanted to get all Chuck Norris on them and punch them in the throat. I couldn't control time, so I wanted that theory to die. I rushed through the healing process like a banshee and celebrated each month that went by, because to me it signified that I was that much better.

Then one night I had a dream that we were still married and actually happy. Talk about a tailspin. I was *furious* that I had a setback, that I couldn't stop thinking about him. I cried and frantically called my therapist. *"What the hell is this?!"* I asked her. And she ever so calmly told me, "Remember when I told you the grief process is a process? You go through it over and over again, possibly for years and years to come." Well, that was *not* what I wanted to hear.

However . . . I listened and I surrendered to the feelings. Not right then and there, but over time. Reality was, I had lost a big part of my life. It was the death of a marriage. I am not superhuman; I cannot control my grief. And I cannot speed up time, try though I did. Once I let all that go, it got easier.

Keep Yourself Busy

Left alone with nothing but boredom and time, the mind can wander; we can start feeling like a victim and depressed, start scheming up ways to get him back, start plotting revenge or other unhealthy shenanigans. The best thing to do post breakup is take out your calendar and start filling it up. Call all those people you've been meaning to call, start that new exercise thing you've been wanting to do, cook meals you've never cooked, volunteer where your heart tells you to, anything.

An add-on to this idea is to make plans for your future. Set goals, break them down into manageable steps, and plan them out. Strategize and list out your "Hell yeses." What do you want to do that you weren't able to do when you were attached? This is your opportunity to do what *you* want.

Look at the Experience as a Gift

This might sound like the stupidest thing you've ever heard, especially if you're in the depths of your breakup, but hear me out. A change in perspective has the ability to move mountains. What if you could itemize what you've learned from this experience? You might be thinking, "Well, I learned that he's a major asshole." That's fine, but I want you to focus on *you*. Ask yourself:

- What did you learn about you?
- What did you learn about relationships?
- What did you learn about what you will and will not tolerate?
- What circumstances, feelings, thoughts, or beliefs do you need to own?

If all you come up with are not-so-nice things about yourself, follow up each of those "learnings" with, "Is that really true?" For example, if you think that what you learned is that you're just bad at relationships, challenge that self-doubt with, "Am I 100% sure that is true?" My point is to think critically about the experience and take from it what you can do to become a better you.

Don't Allow Your Ex to String You Along

Your ex may send you mixed signals or be undecided about what he wants. And you and your heart get bounced around like a Ping-Pong ball. Your ex may very well be confused, but he's also getting his ego rubbed by you sticking around pining for him while he figures out if he wants to be with you or not. Leave his ass. No one who loves you for real would do that to you. He may be a master at giving you one glimmer of hope that sooner or later he'll want to be with you, but in the meantime it's your heart that is being abused, neglected, and disrespected. Total deal breaker. Choose what's best for you, not what's best for him.

Stop Sleeping with Your Ex

It still baffles me to no end when a woman is still sleeping with her ex, and is under the impression that this is the answer to get him back. Truth: He's sleeping with you because you're willing, not because he's thinking about getting back together. I don't care what kind of new tricks you're showing off in the boudoir, he's only in it for the s-e-x. What you're getting is confusion, false hope, emotional chaos, and maybe an STD, because he's probably dating other women.

Make Peace with the Fact That You May Never Be 100 Percent over It

Most people never get to a place where they are 100 percent unfeeling about their past relationships. Perhaps it's like scar tissue on their hearts . . . there is a great deal of healing, but there is still some residual sting associated with it. But it doesn't have to mean anything. It doesn't have to mean that you still want to be with your ex, or still have feelings for that person. It just means that you're human, you had an emotional, probably intimate, attachment to this person and that's okay.

It's what you do with those thoughts that counts. If the thoughts of your ex send you tailspinning into grief, or hating yourself for what you did in the relationship or because he broke up with you, that's where it can get dangerous (see Chapter 9). But if you still think of this person and have some minor hurt feelings over it, in my opinion, it's normal.

Allow Yourself to Be (Are You Ready . . .) Alone

(Is Kim Kardashian reading this?) If you're someone who jumps from one relationship to another, listen up. Dig deep and get honest with yourself about why you seem to always be in a relationship. For me, my hit-over-the-head-with-a-brick "aha" moment was admitting I was a love addict (yes, it's a real addiction, not just a Robert Palmer song). It might not be you, but it's worth looking into. It basically means that you're addicted to relationships, the person in the relationship, and/or falling in "love." Love addicts can actually get high from this. It's just that love and relationships are the drug of choice.

Individual autonomy is imperative for a healthy relationship. If your relationships keep failing, perhaps it's time for you to spend some time alone. To get to know yourself without anyone else, to find out what you really want in relationships, your life, your future. Are you in relationships for the sake of being in one? Because being alone is harder? Guuuurl, I've been there. The thing is, you will spend a lifetime looking for "the one," trying to make ill-fated relationships work, and pulling your hair out wondering what the hell is wrong with you or him. The answer is there is nothing wrong with anyone—you don't know yourself yet.

★

There's no way around it, breakups suck. But wallowing in self-pity and acting desperate gets you nowhere, fast. Putting yourself first and deciding what you really want *outside* of your relationship will put you on the path to your best self.

CHAPTER 11

ACCEPT THAT
You'll Have Regrets

We hear it all the time . . . "Don't live your life with regrets!" And as a life coach, I feel it is my duty to preach this as well. Regret can be an awful feeling to live with because 99 percent of the time we can't go back and change things. A decision has been made, and looking back, it may not have been the best one at the time.

I always tell people that if you learned something from it, it's not a regret. Take, for instance, a relationship or marriage that ended. A part of you might be bitter and angry. It might feel like those years were wasted and, quite frankly, you'll probably be pissed about the time gone by and want it back. But in reality, I'm sure there is a long list of things you learned, and if that's the case, you don't need to regret it one bit.

But that's easier said than done. Sometimes when I hear, "Don't live life with regrets," I still feel a little panicked. Because in reality I do have regrets, and you probably do, too.

After my marriage broke up, I met a guy. It was a completely unhealthy relationship, yet it was what I thought I needed at that time. I had gone back to school to finish my bachelor's degree and looked into spending a semester abroad in Australia. I had always wanted to visit and this was the perfect opportunity. I wasn't married, I didn't have kids . . . I felt it was a once-in-a-lifetime trip. I had all the information I needed to sign up, and my student loans would cover it.

But Mr. Unhealthy Relationship didn't want me to go. So I didn't.

To this day, I totally regret this decision. I should have gone. I should have done what my heart was telling me to do. I shouldn't have chosen him over the trip. But I didn't go, and since no one has invented time travel yet, there is nothing I can do about it. Sure, I can travel to Australia in the future, but I can never have that time in my life back with that choice in my hands. And to think that I need to have a life with *no* regrets makes me feel bad about this.

I'm sure you have at least one regret, too: a missed opportunity, a decision you made that you can't take back. Maybe you have an entire list of them. If you do, here are some things to help you get through, and hopefully over, them.

- **Grieve it.** Maybe your regret is that you didn't get to tell someone something so very important before he died. Or you passed up on a job opening that you're seeing now was a major missed opportunity. In other words—it's a *big* one. Take your time to grieve it. Be mad, sad, frustrated, and, well . . . regretful.
- **Learn from it.** Like it or not, we tend to learn something from difficult situations. In my example, I learned that my intuition was right, and that people pleasing never wins. You might learn the same thing from your regret, or something as simple as "I'll never do that again." Whatever it is, the learning is perfect for you.
- **Make peace with it.** You may still be beating yourself up for your regret. Thoughts like, "I was so stupid! I can't believe I did that!" You already know you can't change the past, nor can you change your decision. What you *can* change is how you talk to yourself

about it and how to speak about it out loud to others. Give up the dialogue that goes in circles about what happened.

- **Forgive yourself and accept that that outcome can never be different.** In Chapter 34, I talk about how to forgive yourself for past mistakes. This is imperative here. If you're having a lot of trouble with this one, ask yourself what exactly you're making this regret mean. Are you coming to conclusions about your future because of it? Or are you putting labels on yourself about it (loser, flake, bad decision maker, etc.)?

Remember that most, if not all, of us have regrets at the end of our lives. It's futile to pretend you don't. There comes a time when you just need to call a spade a spade and have a regret or two. Or ten. Everything in your life—even your regrets—have in some way shaped you . . . but you get to determine in what way.

CHAPTER 12

DON'T TAKE
Other People's
Piles of Shit

When someone talks shit to your face or you hear that someone dissed you second hand, it's human nature to be hurt or even angry. If you heard someone doesn't like you, or judged you for something you did (or didn't do!), you probably feel like crap. It stings a little, doesn't it? Or maybe a lot.

It's totally normal and human to want to be accepted by others. And when we are judged or criticized, we might feel rejected. And when we feel rejected, it's hard to accept it—part of us wants to fix it or make it right. To be accepted is to feel loved. But to feel that we are *not* part of a group, or that we have done or said something "wrong," can make us feel like an outcast. Feeling this way can cause our emotions to spiral downward quickly.

Again, all of these feelings are normal, but there's another, healthier way to deal with that kind of situation.

Think about a time when you have judged someone. I'm sure you've done it recently, as we all have in some way or another. For example, say you read a news article about a teenage mother who had her small children taken away for being an unfit parent. Let's say she left them home alone while she went out and partied.

Your thoughts might be, "She should have been using birth control if she was going to make the irresponsible decision to have sex as a teenager." Or, "She should have given those babies up to a more responsible family who *wanted* children." Or, "How could she be so stupid? Where are *her* parents?"

Your opinion is that she is irresponsible and stupid. This is also your judgment of her. It's likely that you are also afraid this could someday be your teenage daughter or another member of your family making these types of decisions about her life. Your judgments are based on *your* opinions, *your* thoughts, and, quite possibly, *your* fears.

You've inadvertently made the situation about you. You *think* it's about her, but you're really dealing with *your* reaction to her decisions. Again: *your* reaction.

So let's get back to you.

Let's say someone says something terrible about you. Or you find out that someone doesn't like you. What if you could be absolutely certain their words had nothing to do with you? That *you knew* that other people's negative thoughts about you are simply reflections of themselves? An example might be that your friend's spouse doesn't like you. Maybe he thinks that you're too forward and outspoken. In this particular situation, I would bet that that person has issues with women who express leadership qualities. That it's *his* own personal insecurities with himself that make him uncomfortable and hence dislike you. So it's really all his issue.

Other people's negative thoughts about you are simply reflections of themselves.

Think about what this could open up for you. You could actually be one of those people who don't give a crap what other people think of them. Those people aren't unicorns. They really *do* exist. And you really can be one of them.

Now getting back to that imaginary person that I mentioned in the beginning of the chapter who said something mean about you. What are the thoughts and feelings behind it for you? Pain? Sadness? Anger? Confusion?

Now, decide that it is a fact that the other person's feelings about you have absolutely nothing to do with you. It has no bearing on your self-worth or who you are as a person. My friend and colleague, Brooke Castillo, explains this brilliantly. She said other people's opinions are good for other people and that *you* are the constant here. If other people's opinions were right about you, everyone's opinion would be the same about you . . . because again, you are the constant. She says to pay the closest attention to the opinion that matters the most: yours. If you're having trouble even fathoming this notion, look at it from this angle: You are giving this other person a lot of power. You're just handing it over sheepishly, as if it rightly belongs to him or her. And it doesn't.

My best friend and colleague, Amy Smith, has a metaphor that I love to think of when this topic comes up. She asks, "If someone had a big pile of shit in their arms and tried to give it to you, would you take it? Or would you say 'No, thank you. That's *your* pile of shit and I don't want it.'" Sounds about right, wouldn't you say?

Now, what if you think of other people's opinions, judgments, and criticisms in the same way? It's their pile of shit, and you have the choice whether to take it from them or not.

Duh. Don't take it!

CHAPTER 13

TAKE INVENTORY
of Your Nonnegotiables

Nonnegotiables are the tangible things that when you don't have them in your life, you feel lost, unbalanced, unfulfilled, and unhappy. These things are sacred to you, in big ways or small. An easy example here might be that you need your morning coffee the way you like it. If something goes wrong with it, or you don't get it, you might be ready to rip someone's head off. If that's you, your morning coffee would be one of your nonnegotiables. These are tied into your top values (see Chapter 4), but they're the everyday, tangible examples of them.

So why are nonnegotiables important? Because getting clear about who you are and what makes you your best self is why we're all here, right? And if you're your best self, other people understand that you honor yourself and they are more likely to honor you, too.

Let me make that clearer:

1. You know what makes you happy.

2. You do what makes you happy.

3. Other people in your life see this and do the same for you.

4. Other people have more respect for you and your life.

5. The world is a better place.

If you aren't sure what your nonnegotiables are, then how do you find out? First, don't feel bad if you don't know. You've probably been running around, taking care of everyone else for so long, you just don't know yet. Here are a few questions for you to think deeply about (in other words, confer with your heart here and not your head).

- What do you do that makes you feel most alive? The most like *you*?
- What, when missing, makes you simply not feel good?
- When you can't do something you had planned and you feel angry or irritated by the interruption, what you were doing?

If, after reading those questions and trying to answer them, you still have no idea, let's back up a bit. Go back to Chapter 4 and look at your list of values. (This was your list of things that are truly important to you and important about the way you live your life.) In that chapter, I asked you to rate them. Look at the values you rated the highest, meaning that they are very important to you and you live them as best you can every day. Let's say you rated "Physical Environment" a nine. Maybe you love the community you live in, or your bedroom is decorated exactly how you like it. A nonnegotiable action for you might be that every day you get to spend time there. It doesn't have to be a big, monumental action. It can be something small like that. (And who knows, maybe the reason you've had your panties in a bunch lately is because one of the important values you thought was being honored isn't right now. It'll be like a long-lost lover coming home when you prioritize it.)

Some of your nonnegotiables could also be one or two of the values that you rated low, so look at those, too. There might be something small you can do to start improving that value's rating.

For example, right now, my nonnegotiables are:

- Exercising (which is usually running *alone*).
- Coffee the way I like it in the morning.
- Some time during the week to write.

Notice, none of these things include anyone else. If your nonnegotiables do, that's fine—but keep in mind that you can't rely on other people, so just be careful. I know many people who have family and friends on their list. And just because none of mine involved my children or husband doesn't mean I don't like spending time with them, it's just that these nonnegotiables should only be about *you*. It's not selfish or self-absorbed to make them a priority.

Three of your nonnegotiables need to happen in your life on a regular basis. There's really no good reason on earth that can't happen.

It's a choice. That's all. Choose to commit to your top nonnegotiables. It might mean saying no to extra work with your kids' school or your church. If you're having trouble fitting them in, schedule these things into your days as if they were very important appointments, like getting a pap smear or picking up your kid from school. Although I'm sure your nonnegotiables are way more fun than getting a pap smear.

These sometimes change over time, maybe even change every week. It doesn't matter or make them any less important if they do.

Make them happen.

CHAPTER 14

SHUT UP and Listen

I think I just heard you say, *"What?"*

Human brains are entirely too smart.

Now, I'm not accusing you of being the type of person who is *never* really listening to the person you're having a conversation with (and if you are, this may be the reason all your friends have given you the heave-ho). This is merely a reminder that fundamentally we all want one very big, important thing from other people:

To be seen and heard.

I am familiar with this situation because I used to be the queen of arguments. Not only that, but when I was arguing, I would barely hear what the other person was saying. I was so busy wanting to be right, wanting to win, wanting to say the most witty, sarcastic rebuttal that I had little time to listen and hear what the other person was saying.

And I think there might be one or two other people out there like me. Given that, let's all shoot for effective and healthy communication. And that starts with really listening.

I'm not trying to be an asshole here and patronize you by any means. We live in a fast-paced culture where everything is a race. But human connection, communication, and conversation should not be one of them.

Over the years I've learned: If you really, truly want to show that you care about someone, and you really do give a crap about the words that are coming out of his or her mouth, give your undivided attention and *listen*. And for bonus points, pause before you reply.

Listening shows that you have respect for each other and are showing up in the relationship. Think of what you are missing by not really, truly listening to the people you love and care about. Here are some steps to follow.

1. The next time you're having a conversation, when you notice your own mind wandering off into space, or the grocery store, or Tahiti, or wherever, just come back.

2. If you're in a disagreement, you probably start to rehearse your rebuttal as the other person is talking (or shouting). Stop doing that. Stop and really listen to that person even if you think what he's saying is the stupidest thing you have ever heard. Instead, take a second or two to replay in your mind what he just said. Or, if you weren't listening (ahem), ask him to repeat it. Again, *even if you think it's the stupidest thing you've ever heard.* I know, it's difficult. Practice it.

3. Next, practice reflective listening. It goes like this: Someone tells you something; it could be a problem, an issue, anything. When he is finished speaking, you tell him what you heard. Don't repeat it word-for-word, because that will just piss him off, but tell him in your own words what you heard. It might start with, "This is what I'm hearing you say: You're frustrated with me because you feel that I . . ."

If you're not listening effectively with meaning to the other person, then your arguments are just words flying around the air. And we all know that we don't need any more pollution. Being a good listener is a great way to show you care and love someone. And everyone wants that, right?

One final communication tip: Come out and ask the person what it is that he really wants. Many of us have the same arguments time and time again and *we* don't even know what we want. We keep arguing because we're not *really* asking for what we want, so we never get it. We're arguing around the issue.

Next time, ask yourself what it is you really want and try to articulate it. When I have disagreements with my husband, sometimes I find myself blaming and trying to prove my point, when what I really want from him is to help me with something. Or I just need a hug. But trying to be right sends me off course and I never ask for what I want.

So, in summary:

- Pause and truly listen before you decide what to say next.
- Reflect back what you just heard in your own words.
- Clearly and respectfully ask for what you want.
- Don't forget to keep being your kick-ass self.

CHAPTER 15

HAVE MORE FUN

When you hear the phrase "Have more fun," what comes to mind? Do you see having fun as being childish, irresponsible, or careless? Or do you think that you're too busy for fun? "I *really* don't have time. Me having fun would just be selfish. I have too much to do."

Is there really no room for fun in your life? Even if you could really use a laugh?

For the sake of this chapter, I'm referring to the times you feel overwhelmed with life. For example, the following are all crystal clear indicators that it's time to get some belly laughs in, get off your ass, and just generally enjoy more of life:

- When your focus becomes narrow and your to-do list feels like the be all and end all of your existence.
- When something *feels* like a really big deal, but when you sit down to really think about it, it's not.
- When you flat out think to yourself, "I wish I was having more fun."

(I'm not saying that if you're in a place of serious despair or grief, it's time to watch hilarious YouTube videos or make jokes about your situation. Absolutely not! Honor your feelings at times like those.)

I don't need to give you scientific stats of how having fun makes people healthier, more beautiful, blah, blah, blah. I would bet mucho dinero you already know that having fun makes you feel happier and freer. I don't care if you're an uber-serious, buttoned-up investment banker. Or a constipated librarian (no offense, librarians). Having fun is within every single person, including you.

The thing about life, and especially about personal development, is sometimes it can seem to get pretty damn serious. When things get deep and we have moments of self learning, many times there are tears. Trust me, I know. In my opinion, if you're not learning at least some of the time, you're not living, At the same time, a lot of learning about your life and yourself can seem pretty serious. Don't let all that seriousness and hard work bog you down. Laugh a little. Having fun gives you distance from, and maybe some perspective on, a problem you're having. It reminds you of what's right in the world. You can have fun in five minutes or five hours, whatever you've got.

Maybe you have no idea if you need more fun in your life or not. Let's start there and answer these questions:

- On a scale of one to ten, with ten being the most, how much fun are you having on a regular basis (on average)?
- Do you think at the end of your life you might say, "I wish I had had more fun"?
- Are you envious of other people that are having fun?

Your answers probably gave you an indicator of where you are.

So, ask yourself . . . what's fun *to you*?

This in itself is a loaded topic. I'm not here to give you a list of things that are fun, because fun tastes vary widely.

Keep in mind that what is fun for someone else might not be fun for you. Be honest about what you find fun and beware of "shoulds" here. You having fun isn't about pleasing anyone but *you*. It's okay if other people don't get your kind of fun, or they think it's weird. Those people don't have to adopt your "funness."

And for some people, fun is an acquired taste. In other words, they need to really dig into something, practice it, give it time to get really good at it before they would consider it really fun. Other people might find something fun from the start, and as they get proficient in it, they get disenchanted with it and the fun-factor is gone. Neither way is wrong or right. The point is to find your fun and have it!

CHAPTER 16

DUMP THE FRIENDS
You've Outgrown

Mentally or on paper, list out your top five friends. Now put stars by the ones you feel have a mutual commitment to the friendship—those who reciprocate respect and support and all the other things that are important to *you*.

Yes, this *is* sort of like, "Well, Jane is my first best friend. Candace is my second best friend . . . " and so on. Don't worry; they don't need to know where they score.

Look at the people who don't have stars. Who are they? And why are they on your list?

The reasons could vary. Either you've been friends since first grade and just feel bad thinking about leaving that person behind, or this person saw you through a really tough time and you "owe" it to her to stick around.

First of all, you're not playing hopscotch anymore. And you're not wearing the same clothes from 1982, so why are you holding on to the friendship? Probably you *both* feel the same way, just one of you needs to grow some balls and exit. And secondly, you don't "owe" anything to the person who was there for you. As long as you have thanked the person for being a good friend, that's sufficient.

Let's say you have an old, beat-up car that keeps breaking down, even though you have the money to actually buy a new car. But you've had the car for fifteen years; it's been with you through so many events in your life so you keep it around for nostalgic reasons. Plus, the car buying process itself is such a hassle. Still, after so many stuck-on-the-side-of-the-road episodes, you would wise up and get yourself a new ride, right? The same thing can apply to friendships. Why the hell are you still going shoe shopping and having lattes with this woman who is dragging you down? There is absolutely *no* reason you need to give that friendship any more time and energy.

If you do an inventory at the end of your life, I'm sure you're not going to want to see, "2003–2017: Held onto friendship that was long expired. Wasted 2,458 hours of life." Major bummer.

You are not responsible for these people. It's not up to you to hold onto them for fear of hurting their feelings. You never know—maybe they're at home right now thinking the same thing and holding onto *you* because they don't want to hurt *you*.

You know in your gut if the friendship is expired. Because here's the truth: people evolve, change, and grow as life goes on. Marriages begin and some end, children might be born, and jobs change. When people change, certain friendships can't withstand the change. It says nothing bad about the two people in the relationship. No one needs to be the one who was "wrong," or the mean girl for ending it; no one is "better" or "worse." It doesn't have to mean anything. It's just a relationship that ended and the best part is that both people can be better for the sheer fact that the relationship has existed. The friendship served its purpose in its time, but now there's no longer a need for it. Both parties now have room to grow, and can find extra energy to be used for something or someone else.

So you're probably wondering, *How the hell do I end a friendship?* Ending a friendship can be just as hard as breaking up with an intimate partner, so you're totally normal if you feel really sad and uncomfortable. There are two ways to go about ending the friendship:

1. The first way is to have a mature conversation about it. However, chances are that if the friendship has become dysfunctional or weak, the breakup conversation may not go well. Brace yourself for perhaps some manipulation, Facebook slandering, and other drama. As painful as that would all be, it would be your definitive evidence of why the friendship should be over. A face-to-face talk is always best, where feelings can be expressed as clearly as possible, but if you feel strongly about using e-mail instead, do that. No matter how you tell the person, avoid blaming and try your best to come from a place of love and compassion.

2. The other way is to slowly let the friendship die on its own. Stop making plans with her and stop forcing the relationship. Eventually it will just shut down. Your friend may or may not contact you asking what's going on, and if she does, tell her the truth.

Bottom line: whichever way will make you proud of yourself is the route you should go. If you can stand with integrity in the situation, you know you've ended things in the best way possible.

There is no reason in the world you need to be tolerating a friendship (or any relationship!) that doesn't fill you up, empower you, inspire you, and make you a better person. An unfulfilling friendship that has been going on for too long is essentially life clutter you need to clean out.

CHAPTER 17

PAIN = Wisdom

Everyone has pain. Everyone has sustained heartbreak. If there was a pill for getting over heartbreak, it would sell on the black market for thousands and/or a big pharmaceutical company would own it, and most of the world. Everyone has a painful story that would at least bring tears, if not bring you to your knees. Everyone has pain—what separates people is what they do with that pain. You can choose to let it define you, or you can choose to recreate yourself.

Basically, you have two choices:

1. Stay in pain.
2. Gain any available wisdom and insight and start to move forward.

In option one, there is no relief. You've been dealt a shitty card, your circumstances are painful, and you choose to stay there. It's an entrée of feeling sorry for yourself with a side of blaming others, and for dessert, stay in the sad story that this is your destiny. Your fate. Boo hoo.

In option two, you've still been dealt a shitty card; your circumstances are still painful. But the difference is that you shift perspectives and reflect on what you've learned.

So what are your painful experiences? What is the thing that influenced your life so greatly that it still stings to think about or talk about? Chances are, you know it right away. The best way to help yourself move on is to write down everything you've learned from it. Ask yourself important, introspective questions about your pain and explore how you can use it to serve you better. Pull yourself out of the story for a few minutes and look at what the gift is. It doesn't mean you aren't in pain anymore. It just means you're strong enough to use it as a tool for growth.

Here are some examples of gaining insight from painful experiences:

Perhaps you made a bad decision. Perhaps you got pregnant "by accident" while in a relationship with some guy you desperately loved, with the intention that the baby would help the relationship. (I know this has *never, ever* happened in real life, but bear with me here.) Shockingly, he left you and the baby and you're understandably heartbroken. The wisdom you might find is that you realize you need to look at why you wanted so desperately to hold on to him in the first place. Or you reflect on the fact that you do need to be alone to decide what you really want for your life.

Perhaps someone you love tragically died. What did he teach you while he was alive? What piece of him do you want to take with you into your daily life?

Or maybe someone did something terrible to you. What did you learn about yourself? What will you not tolerate again?

Yes, we all have failures, heartbreak, and emotional pain, but it's not *who* we are. It's just circumstances and facts. *No one* is destined for failure. *No one* is destined to be heartbroken. And circumstances do not determine who you are, your worth, or your future.

You're responsible for all of that.

If you find it too hard to figure out what you learned from your painful experience, I'd like to know why you're so committed to staying in pain? Why do you think you need to stay here? Try to see the other side of the coin.

Pretty soon, it won't be so painful anymore.

CHAPTER 18

FIND Your Passions

I can't tell you how many times I've heard women tell me they have no idea what their passion, purpose, or life mission is. And who can blame them—identifying a "life mission" sounds so intimidating! (*Fantastic.* Let's add more pressure on women.)

Sarcasm aside, let's look at this for a moment. I've always thought it was crazy to ask sixteen- or seventeen-year-old kids to pick a college major. To actually pick something they want to do as a career. Forever. When I was seventeen, all I wanted to do was pick a cool bodysuit and matching scrunchie to wear. That was about the extent of my vision— it did not include what I wanted to study for four years, and then do as a career. I envied my peers who did know and felt badly about myself that I did not. Clearly there was something wrong with me and I was a flake.

Fast-forward twenty years, and I am on my fifth career. People tell me, "It's so awesome that you've found your thing." In all honesty, this "compliment" makes me feel panicked. Is this my forever thing? My one true life-calling purpose? I think it is . . . but the *one thing* I was put on this earth to do? What if I got it all wrong? How scary is that?!

I've realized that I'm not alone. When it comes to their life calling, people often worry:

1. That their chosen calling isn't "good enough."
2. That they shouldn't ever, ever, *ever* change their mind once they've chosen one.
3. That they haven't found a "real" purpose.

Frankly, all of that is bullshit.

Let's look at each scenario. First, it really bothers me when people go through life panicked that their "thing" doesn't stack up to someone else's. They're afraid it's not important enough, or selfless enough, or *whatever* enough. Just because you're not a bestselling author or traveling the world helping orphans doesn't make you any less of a human being. And it certainly doesn't mean that *you* matter any less.

Maybe your life purpose is that you learn about yourself and the world on this journey of life, you do your best to be a good person and be kind to people, and help some people who need help. The end. Maybe doing those three things for the entire ninety-nine or so years of life is really what you were meant to do.

Second, I firmly believe that many of us won't just have one "thing." And that's okay. Many women feel uneasy if they want to change their mind every few years, afraid that they'll seem uncommitted or flighty. But what if you think something is your "calling," you go after it, and turns out it's not? Oh shit, right? Well . . . maybe not. Imagine for a sec that it's actually no big deal.

Think about it this way: How many times have you bought something from a catalog or online, tried it on, and decided that it wasn't right? On the return form, usually there are boxes that say wrong color, wrong fit, not as pictured, and *changed mind*. It's just not a big deal to them, apparently. Just a box to check.

Bottom line: If you want to change your mind, give yourself a break. Personally, I think it's braver to admit you want to change course and then make it happen than to suffer a passionless life.

Finally, some of us never find a specific vocation or career-based calling. If you're stressing the hell out about that, relax. It doesn't mean you're less of an important person. It doesn't mean you're a failure if you don't find it. All it means is that your purpose might not be something specific that you do. Don't worry:

Who you are and what you represent is purposeful enough.

If you're unsure where to even start finding a life purpose, ask yourself this:

What is that thing you love doing?

You know, the thing you can get lost in and lose track of time. The thing that in a perfect world you could make a living doing (and P.S. It's possible. Just sayin'.). Is there something you love to read about, research, and find out everything you can about it?

Maybe it's something you used to do as a kid but haven't in a while for whatever reason. I started writing as a kid and wrote all through my teen years. In my twenties, I stopped. When I picked it back up in my early thirties, I had no idea how much I had missed it. It was as if the floodgates had opened. I gorged on writing. Even if you think it's silly, try to reconnect with those things you used to do as a child.

Or maybe it's not a "thing" you have but a message. Take a moment to imagine you're with an enormous group of people sitting in front of an empty stage. Suddenly there is an announcement that *you* will be giving a thirty-second speech to the crowd. You have thirty seconds to tell everyone what's in your heart. What will you say to them?

Here's another angle. Many times people feel a calling toward, and become passionate about, the very thing that has caused them pain and suffering. Hard times can be pivotal points that shape us and make us stronger. What if you could help people who are dealing with the same circumstances you once did? Or help create awareness and become an advocate for a particular condition or situation? Many times, these opportunities are right in front of our faces.

Keep in mind that whether you find your passion or purpose today, next month, or in ten years, it's the right time for you. The timing and the process of it all is your own unique recipe.

CHAPTER 19

LOVING YOURSELF
Is the New Black

You know that person everyone falls in love with the second he or she walks into a room? He or she doesn't necessarily have to be gorgeous, or start throwing cash around the room? No, this person just has "something" that draws others in. And you'd give your right arm to know *what* it is that is so super awesome about that person. She isn't necessarily even charming or charismatic; she just seems to radiate something that is magnetic.

I'll save you the endless nights awake trying to figure out what it is. Truth: That person loves herself. The end.

Confidence is about believing in yourself. Self-esteem is about believing in your worth.

Self-love is both of those wrapped up into one, plus more. It's like the perfect feast for your soul.

And at the same time, self-love can be this mysterious, elusive thing. Ask a woman what her menstrual cycle is like or how she takes her coffee and she can tell you in great detail. But ask her about self-love and you'll probably get a blank stare.

If you're not sure whether you love yourself, here's a quick quiz:

1. Do you think you're awesome?
2. Do you love yourself unconditionally? (In other words, do you put conditions on your self-love such as your weight, salary, relationship status, etc.?)
3. Do you go after your goals while deep down knowing you are worthy of attaining them?

If you answered "no" to any or all of these questions, we've got some work to do, sister!

What *is* self-love anyway? In a nutshell, it's embracing your imperfect self. It's:

- Forgiving yourself for any past mistakes and moving forward.
- Forgiving others.
- Not contingent on your particular circumstances, how much pain you're in, what you look like, or how much money you have.
- Not believing the made-up stories your inner critic might tell you.

In my humble opinion, self-love is the best thing ever.

Yet, in our culture, self-love is such a misunderstood concept. Self-love is *not* conceited, narcissistic, self-absorbed, or vain. If you think that's the case, I want you to scratch that record and create a new definition of self-love. One that starts with accepting who and where you are right now in this moment, no matter what is happening in or around you. No matter what you've been through in the past.

So let's do it. Make the decision right now to love yourself. Think it in your head; say it out loud. It might feel uncomfortable at first, but remember . . . anything worth fighting for has the tendency to be uncomfortable. And you are absolutely worth fighting for.

You might be thinking, "Is it really that easy? I just make the decision?"

Well, yes and no.

Yes, you can say those words to yourself. But no, it's not like magic where you suddenly find yourself running through a field of daisies with your arms wide open (or if you do, you're in a tampon commercial). Remember (from Chapter 1), your thoughts create your feelings and, in the end, your reality. So why not choose the best thoughts that will bring you the best life? You want to choose positive thoughts that come from a place of love in your heart, not the fearful thoughts that are in your head.

Here's another great thing about self-love: When you love yourself, the right people will be attracted to you and show up in your life. Self-love is some sort of magnetic energy that isn't tangible, but people feel something great about you. Other people with good thoughts and good energy will want to be around you.

It's time to be your own biggest fan, a legend even! You don't have to announce it or have a vanity license plate telling everyone how awesome you think you are. At first, it can be your own little secret. Once you've made the decision to love yourself, here are some actions to take:

- Take responsibility for your life. Notice where you blame others or circumstances for your unhappiness or lack of fulfillment. Forgive people if you need to. Let it go.
- Forgive yourself for your past. You don't live there anymore, so why are you still beating yourself up over it and letting it dictate your own self-love and self-worth?
- Own your story and at the same time love yourself for it. *Everyone* has a messy past. You're human.
- Set healthy boundaries. Stop tolerating toxic people and drama (a.k.a. don't put up with other people's bullshit).
- Go after what you want (step out of your comfort zone if you need to). You'll be scared. Do it anyway.

- Believe you are worth what you want. And I mean everything.
- Take care of your physical, mental, and emotional well-being. Go to the doctor. See a therapist or counselor. Allow people to help you.
- Accept praise and compliments. Those are gifts. Say thank you instead of downplaying or denying the kind words.

You'll see that many of these themes appear throughout this book. That's because loving yourself is the first step in getting your kick-ass life. If you don't love yourself, it's hard to respect and believe in yourself. It's hard to know you are worth anything. And it's really hard to follow through with goals, to set good intentions, and to step into your destiny.

Yes, your *destiny*. Because I know for a fact it is not your destiny to live a life of wishing and hoping for good things to happen to you. Fingers crossed. Believing dreams only come true for "those people." You know what "those people" have in common? They love themselves.

It's not luck; it's love, baby.

CHAPTER 20

YOU CAN'T "Feel Fat"

Let's have a chat about "fat talk." Fat talk is this conversation we have with ourselves or others, particularly women. Do any of these sound familiar?

- *You look great! Have you lost weight?*
- *I'm too fat to wear this.*
- *I can't believe I just pigged out.*
- *She shouldn't be wearing that.*
- *I was really bad today and ate pizza.*
- *I can only wear that if I lose ten pounds.*

This is fat talk. Most women (and men, too) are guilty of it. I believe this type of talk has become so normal and comfortable for us that we don't even realize it's happening when we say it or when we hear it from others. My hope is you will start to notice you might be doing it and/or hearing it.

Even sadder is that the thoughts don't stop with just sentences about our bodies. Many times they are followed up with a frantic to-do list of what we must do in the next week so we can "fix" the problem. This list often includes things like: Start working out again, only eat X amount of calories per day, go shopping for Spanx, download a calorie counting app, start weighing yourself every morning, and on and on and on.

Think about this for a minute—what is this conversation doing to us? Making us happier? Helping us lose weight? Making our relationships and friendships stronger and richer?

No. It's destroying us.

It's a cycle that starts out detrimental to our souls and ends with disappointment, thus recreating the cycle over and over again.

Let's change the conversation. Let's not bond over the commiseration of the way our bodies look. Let's not associate looking good with weight loss. Instead of, *"You look great, have you lost weight?"* How about just a good, old-fashioned, *"You look amazing!"* Period.

Fat talk is not limited to conversations we have with others. Fat talk is often the conversation we have with ourselves. In 2011, *Glamour* magazine asked 300 young women of all sizes to record every negative or anxious thought they had about their bodies for one day. Their research found that, on average, women have thirteen negative body thoughts daily—nearly one for every waking hour. And a disturbing number of women confessed to having thirty-five, fifty, or even 100 hateful thoughts about their own shapes each day. A whopping 97 percent admitted to having at least one "I hate my body" moment.

This, my friends, is tragic.

How many times have you thought or said, "I feel fat"? I have heard the words come out of my mouth too many times to count.

But the last time I checked, fat is not a feeling. You can't "feel fat."

When you find yourself saying that, ask yourself what *else* you are feeling or what the *real* underlying feeling is. Uncomfortable? Unmotivated? Confused? Unhealthy? Not yourself?

Those are all valid feelings and get to the root of what's really happening in your thoughts. Because, as you should know by now, your feelings are dictated by your thoughts, not your circumstances.

If you're having trouble avoiding fat talk right off the bat, simply *notice* how often you hear it at first. Gradually start pulling back and not contributing to conversations about it, using the tools and exercises in this book. Then stop thinking those thoughts.

One great way to move away from fat talk is to focus on intrinsic attributes instead of external ones—not only in yourself, but in other people. Focus on behaviors, talents, passions, skills, uniqueness, etc. If you made a list of your ten favorite things about your best friend, I highly doubt that her weight would be on that list.

CHAPTER 21

MANAGE
Your Inner Critic

You have one, I have one, Oprah has one. We all have an inner critic. It's that voice in our head that tells us various statements about the way we look, about how we measure up to everyone else, about what we're capable (or not capable) of doing, and so on.

Your inner critic can vary. Sometimes it might simply be disempowering, telling you that the big thing you really want to do is too hard, too expensive, you're too old—in other words, it fuels your excuses. Or it can be a downright nasty bully and tell you you're fat, stupid, and not worthy of love, success, or anything else you truly desire.

I believe these inner critic voices are addicted to suffering. They're addicted to keeping you exactly where you are (even if you're unhappy), keeping you afraid of change, keeping you stuck in indecision. Your inner critic is the majority of the reason you use the word "but" when you say:

- *"I would love to find a different job . . . but it's so much work to look."*
- *"I'm not happy in this relationship . . . but it's probably the best I can do."*

The biggest personality trait of an inner critic is fear. Think about a time when you were afraid to do something, whether it was going for a new job, asking someone out, or trying something new. Your fear manifests as a conversation in your mind. It can sound like this:

- *"What if I look stupid?"*
- *"What if it doesn't work out?"*
- *"I'm not smart enough to do that."*

I know the inner critic so well because I have one, too. She tells me in so many words that my life is a race to the top; I have to do everything perfectly or risk ridicule, shame, and humiliation. When I think of my dreams, she'll tell me they're not possible. She insists that people like me just can't achieve that dream. She says I won't have time, I won't know how, and even if I did, I would do it wrong. In a nutshell, she's a complete and total bitch.

Some people have lived their entire lives listening to this voice as their truth. They have no idea that this idea of an "inner critic" exists and that . . . are you ready?

It can be managed.

The real truth is that you can separate that voice from your true self, and see big shifts in your life. Managing that relationship will help you know your true self and live your kick-ass life with fewer negative interruptions.

The first step in inner critic managing is acceptance. Working on your inner critic is not like getting your tonsils out; it's not going away forever. You'll always have this voice, but you can learn to quiet it.

To start, simply notice when you're lost in inner critic land. It might be right now. Try not to beat yourself up for having this voice in your head. You're simply becoming aware of its presence. Some people notice they are irritated or angry—that they simply don't feel good. Check in to see what the conversation in your head is like during those times. What kind of language are you using with yourself?

Next, question the inner critic's assumptions and "truths." When you find yourself thinking, "I'm such a failure at this," ask yourself, "Is this true?" *Really* ask yourself if you know without a doubt that you are 100 percent certain you are a failure at this. Or has your inner critic convinced you of it? The inner critic is excellent at presenting itself as truth; that's something it has perfected over the years it has lived inside your head. Staying paralyzed in indecision is a clear sign your inner critic voice is keeping you stagnant, so getting clarity on all these "what ifs" will help you decide.

Staying paralyzed in indecision is a clear sign your inner critic voice is keeping you stagnant.

And if you're feeling up to it, changing your perspective around how you look at this inner critic is, of course, your choice. What if you looked at it from a place of compassion? Imagine that it's trying its best to help you, but having a really hard time. Its job is supposed to be protecting you and encouraging you, but it just can't seem to get it right. If this were a person you cared about, you would probably feel bad for him or her (and maybe a little annoyed and that's okay, too). But you may find the inner critic loses its power when you do think of it kind of sucking at its true job. Protectors shouldn't make you feel like shit. Ever.

This work takes practice. No one is able to manage their inner critic overnight. Be persistent in recognizing and questioning those negative inner critic thoughts, and you'll be well on your way.

CHAPTER 22

For the Love of All That Is Holy: *STOP DIETING!*

The diet industry in America rakes in about $55 *billion* a year on weight loss products.

Fifty-five fucking billion dollars, y'all.

Let's take a trip to Fantasyland. Imagine for a moment there were no diet products. No billboards telling you how to finance your liposuction. No diet pills, no diet shakes, and no companies making money off you counting points every time you swallow your food.

No magazines, commercials, or any other ad making you think being thin is the answer to all of your problems. Nothing that makes fat = bad and unhappy, and thin = good and happy.

Just pretend it doesn't exist.

It's like Xanadu, right? An alternate Universe . . . with unicorns farting rainbows.

Here's the hard truth: No matter how much someone or a company promises you'll lose weight, no matter how desperate you are to feel better or different about yourself, no matter how much you hate your body right now:

Diets are bullshit and they don't work.

Diets are about making you "good" or "bad." They make a profit if and only if you "fail" and have to start again.

There's a secret tool out there that the diet industries don't tell you about. Because if you put it into use for yourself, they would lose that $55 billion.

It's called: *Listening to yourself and your own body and loving it along the way.*

Imagine *that*. Say hello to your alternate Universe.

Stop looking for an outside solution here. Stop looking for the magic pill. Stop throwing money at the "problem." The only problem is that as a culture we've turned against the one tool we've had all along. *Your* body knows the answer and can tell you if you just stop for one minute and shut the hell up about how hard it is.

Work on believing you are not broken or need fixing. If you believe you are broken, then the ad companies have gotten a hold of you and done their job. You are perfect as you are, no matter what you weigh at this moment.

When you diet and lose weight, you're skipping the most important part: figuring out the reasons why you overeat and turned to food in the first place. Instead of beating yourself up and looking for action steps to "fix" and change your body, simply be kind and compassionate to yourself and get curious about what's happening when you're taking the action that is making you gain weight.

I know "being kind and compassionate" with yourself may sound somewhat contradictory to "living a kick-ass life," but here's a secret: *It's foundational.* No woman lives a kick-ass life by being a bitch to herself, by thinking she's broken and needs fixing, or by punishing herself. It doesn't work that way.

So if you're on yet another diet, I have to ask: *Why?*

If you answer with "Because I'm overweight" or "Because I've gained weight," again, I want to know why. What's happening in your life that has absolutely nothing to do with food or exercise? What is that thing you don't want to tell anyone because you're afraid? What is the conversation that is happening in your head that makes you eat food you really aren't hungry for?

Because it's not about the diet, it's about you.

And while we're talking about dieting, let's talk about your bathroom scale. Generally speaking, there is an incredible amount of power given to numbers. People like to measure things. They like logistical, practical, black-and-white, tangible numbers. And certain numbers are emotionally charged.

You might be attached to the numbers you see on the scale if you've ever experienced one or more of the following things:

- Have you ever stepped on the scale, looked down at the number, and felt like shit about yourself because of the number you saw?
- Have you ever bargained with yourself about your weight—only doing nice things for yourself when you reach a certain weight?
- Have you ever measured your self-worth based on these numbers?

By now, you probably understand that your thoughts are creating your feelings. It's your thoughts about what you see on the scale that are determining you feeling like shit or feeling great.

And there is absolutely, positively no reason your feelings about yourself should be measured by simply the mass of your physical body. It is your birthright to feel nothing but love for yourself in every way. The number on your scale is just that: a number.

Think about this: Have you ever taken your temperature and seen it higher than normal? Or perhaps your blood pressure at the doctor's office? If these numbers are higher, how do you feel about yourself? Do you fall into self-loathing? Get really angry at yourself? Probably not. So, what if your weight was the same way?

I invite you to throw away your scale. Or donate it. Or take a sledgehammer to it. What if it wasn't in your home anymore, what would that free up for you? *Why* do you think you need it? And if you really feel you're so attached to it, you can't get rid of it, you should take a good, hard look at why. Is it a healthy reason?

I've heard the argument, "But I like to measure where my weight is to track my fitness progress."

I call BS.

There are other ways to measure your fitness. The easiest being how your clothes fit. Or better yet, how you *feel*.

Imagine that?

If you are taking the time and energy to move your body and honor your body by being active, your body will honor you back by *telling you* how it feels. You just need to stop and listen. Have you ever done this?

Right now, take inventory of how your body feels. Are your neck and shoulders tight? Is your jaw clenched? How is your skin? Are you sleeping well? How are your bowel movements? Yep, I just asked you how your poops are.

All of those things are signals of your body's health. The number on the scale can't tell you how well your body is functioning overall. Your body is communicating with you all day, every day—listen to it. Your body will tell you when it's tired, hungry, full, stressed, or restless. Responding to these requests will help you maintain a healthy weight much better than any fad diet ever will.

So do me a favor. Get rid of your scale today. And while you're at it, ditch the dieting drama that goes along with it.

CHAPTER 23

DON'T BE
a Control Freak

Believe me, control freaks always lose. It takes one to know one. I remember sitting on the couch in my therapist's office with my then husband and she called me out.

"You're a control freak," she said. I had a mouth-falls-open-huge-eyes-gasping reaction. How *dare* she say such a thing! But then my intuition sighed and nodded.

It was true. It was one of the million reasons my marriage sucked, along with the fact that I was unhappy, anxiety-ridden, and addicted to whatever my numbing agent du jour was at the time. The bottom line for me was if everyone would just do and act as I said, everything would be fine. Great, even.

Not sure if this is you? Here's a little checklist:

- Control addicts believe that if someone else would change one or two things about him or herself, everyone would benefit (especially the one controlling). So they try to "help others" by pointing out their perceived flaws. Usually over and over. And they make it look like constructive criticism.

- They have unrealistic expectations and in order to make them happen they micromanage others.
- They don't believe in imperfection and don't think anyone else should, either.
- They have a hard time not knowing something and have their hands in many cookie jars at the same time.
- They manipulate others by presenting the worst-case scenario. In other words, they scare the shit out of people in order to get what they want.

(I don't know about you, but the above list doesn't sound like anyone I want to spend time with. Yet at one time I could check off all those things about myself.)

And no matter who you are, here's a list of things you are NOT in control of, and never will be no matter how hard you try:

- The weather
- Other people's feelings
- Other people's words
- Other people's personalities
- Other people's opinions
- Other people's judgments
- Other people's problems
- Other people's actions

Are you noticing a trend here?

People are the way they are. You never filled out a job application to be in charge of their feelings, actions, opinions, etc. So, why, why, why do you try to control it or them?

If you checked off some of those traits above, ask yourself: Is this fun? Is it peaceful to live like this? You may have lived like this for so long you weren't even aware you are doing it, or maybe you do know it, but you just don't know how to live any other way.

It's my opinion that people who live to control are doing it to meet a need. Grasping at straws to create order in their life because deep inside they are suffering. Perhaps they know what the suffering is about, or maybe they don't. But what I do know is that making it your career to control is not going to solve your problems. The suffering will stay. The façade of control is like putting a Band-Aid on a gushing wound.

The good news is that, piece by piece, you can peel back the layers, start to let go, and look inward to see what's really going on.

Ready?

Ask yourself this: Do you like to be free? Do you like the feeling of freedom? I would assume that you do. No one likes to be in bondage, to feel trapped.

Paradoxically, if you try to control other people, if you try to change them in any way, you are essentially holding *yourself* in a place of bondage. You're trapping yourself in a no-win situation.

So, do you want to "win"? Or do you want to be free?

Because even if everyone acted the way *you* think is "right"; if the people you think are making the wrong decisions made what you think are the "right" decisions, would that make you perfectly happy? Or again, are there other issues going on that you're not facing? (See Chapter 25 if you're not sure.)

There's a way for you to be free: Accept the fact that people are the way they are. Is it heartbreaking that someone you love is a drug addict? Yes. Does it piss you off that your coworker sucks at her job? Probably. Do you hate your father-in-law's political views? Maybe. *But it is not your job to control any of this.* Just because you accept it, doesn't mean you have to agree with it, or even understand it. It just means that you choose to be free.

What if you took this perspective: What if other people's journey is simply their journey? One that has neither "good" nor "bad" choices?

I mean, who are you to judge what is really good or bad? What if you could accept that concept? Try it on for size.

The only things you have 100 percent control over are your thoughts. Work on them. Notice where you try to control things, situations, and people. Practice letting it go. Try this mantra, "This is what it is, and I have no control over it. How can I feel better about this?" and go from there. You don't have to feel perfect or even happy about a situation you have no control over, just better.

For example, say your boyfriend or husband has a motorcycle and you're not happy about him riding it. Maybe it's one of *his* nonnegotiables and he won't budge. In this situation, the ball really is in your court. You can accept that he rides his motorcycle and work on letting it go, or leave him. I know it sounds drastic, but those really are your choices. Do whatever *you* need to do to make yourself feel better. Try the simple mantra of "let it go" to yourself when you find yourself getting all worked up about it. It probably will take some real work on your end in order to make this happen, but it *is* possible.

Because let's face it: You like to win. And letting it go will *always* ensure that you do.

CHAPTER 24

DITCH
the Drama Addiction

You know that person who always has some sort of crisis going on? The person who makes a mountain out of a molehill? The person who seems to bring endless drama into any situation?

Oh, wait. Is that you?

If it is, keep reading. This chapter is for both the Queens of Chaos and those around them.

Unnecessary drama and chaos will cut years off of your life (no, that's not an official medical diagnosis, just my own professional opinion) and will make things just plain miserable.

Sure, there are times when shit *goes down*, *Real Housewives*–style, and there is drah-ma. But on an average day, what I'm talking about are the people who jump to conclusions, go from zero to ten on the "Calm to Crisis" scale in two hot seconds, will not let anything go, thrive on gossip, and basically feel uncomfortable in a state of calmness, therefore weaving drama into anything and everything.

I'm exhausted just thinking about her.

Here's one truth about these types of people: They love audiences. Without an audience it's sort of, "If a tree falls in the woods and no one is around, does it make a sound?" But for the Queen of Chaos it's, "If something happens and no one makes a much bigger deal of it, does it really exist?"

Still not sure if you have this person in your life? If you have described someone in the following way . . .

- *"She exhausts me."*
- *"Don't tell her about this because she'll turn it into a much bigger deal than it is."*
- *"I can only handle her in small doses because of all the drama."*

Chances are that person is someone you want to limit your time with.

Unless drama and chaos are two of your personal values (see Chapter 4), it will benefit you to not have these people in your life much. Why, you ask? Because too much drama and chaos causes stress and anxiety, and is just generally unhealthy.

So, what to do?

First, this isn't about her (or him) being "wrong." No blame and shame here. It's simply a matter of *self-care on your behalf.*

That being said, this person may have no idea she's causing so much drama and chaos. It may be so "normal" to her that she's completely oblivious to the fact that she's running around setting fires everywhere while throwing confetti on top of them. So what if you told her? What would be your intention in doing that? Do you truly want to help her? Just make sure you know what *your* intention is. Because remember, you can't, and shouldn't, control other people.

Second, if you have already talked to this person, and she hasn't changed, ask yourself if you really need her in your life. What are *you* holding onto by staying in the relationship? If she is wasting precious energy and time in your life, it's no one's fault but yours (see

Chapter 16). And remember—don't fight fire with fire here. That's fine if you're an MMA fighter, but I'm pretty sure you're not, so this is an opportunity for you to use your skills of *letting it go.* The Queen of Chaos will most likely do her best to reel you back in, so keep your antennae up.

Now for those of you reading who *are* that drama queen: I used to be this girl, too (with an occasional relapse), so I understand. And you may be thinking, "Well, that's just how my life is—dramatic and chaotic." I get that you've created this identity for yourself, but here's the hard truth: Your life's circumstances are probably no more dramatic than anyone else's. People aren't born with the "I-love-creating-and-living-in-drama-and-chaos" gene. It's learned behavior. Probably a coping mechanism to get attention and feel loved—things we all want. You probably don't know any other way and it feels uncomfortable *not* creating drama. Being in a state of calmness feels boring and foreign.

Your life's circumstances are probably no more dramatic than anyone else's.

So start by asking yourself what you're getting out of this behavior. What is it that you're *really* wanting when you create this turmoil? Are you avoiding other things in your life that might be more important by creating distractions (if so, see Chapter 25)?

I'm not asking you to lose your uniqueness—that thing that makes you, you. What I'm asking is for you to find another way for you to connect with others and feel loved. It may be time for you to start asking for what you want. Because when it comes right down to it, it's not about the gossip, the stories, and the assumptions that go with all the drama. That's just what's on the surface. The perceived benefit of getting attention and love from others is really a false one—one that is unhealthy and in the long run will get you nothing but emptiness, thus putting you back at the beginning . . . and you'll end up starting the whole cycle again.

Here's an example of what a situation at work might look like: Say a coworker gave you a weird look when you're getting some coffee . . .

The Queen of Chaos: asks five other people if they saw the look, and what it could possibly mean. Does she think you drink too much coffee? She drinks more coffee than you do, anyway. Does she think your shirt is hideous? Etc., etc.

Reformed Queen of Chaos: wonders if that coworker was having a rough morning; goes about her day normally.

Do you see the major difference? The Reformed Queen of Chaos has won because she is letting go of the notion that the weird look was about her. And can go about the rest of her day without obsessing about something that *really* doesn't matter.

(Also, if you're one of the five people the Queen of Chaos polled, please opt out of the conversation, thus keeping the drama out of your life.)

If nothing else, take a good look here. Avoiding drama might be your ticket to peace, whether you're the instigator yourself or the person on the receiving end.

CHAPTER 25

STOP TRYING TO RUN
Other People's Lives

There's a fine line between trying to help people by giving them advice and trying to tell them what to do—especially if they've been clear about how they feel about your advice in the past (either by not taking it or by telling you straight-up that your advice sucks).

I'm sure we can all relate to being in a situation where we know something is best for someone we care about. We see him clearly doing the wrong thing, going down the wrong path, making the wrong decisions. If only the person would listen to us, his life would be better. It makes us crazy that he won't listen to us, and sometimes it can even negatively affect our own life because we get our panties all in a wad about it.

Just for a minute, keep an open mind for what I'm about to say. You probably think your way is the best way, but again, hang with me for a minute . . .

I ask you: How do you know these decisions are "wrong" for him? Yes, even if your friend is in an abusive relationship and won't leave, or your brother is on drugs and won't get help to quit. In your mind, your advice seems right for that person. But how do you know that what he is going through isn't exactly what he needs?

You might scoff at this and think, "How the hell can being abused or using drugs be exactly where someone needs to be?!" Here's where you need that open mind.

Think of a time when you weren't in a great place and didn't take someone's advice about the situation and you eventually got out of it anyway. A time when you got yourself to a better place mostly by your own free will and decision. Think of the things you learned about yourself during that time. Think of how proud you are that you got out and are in a better place now (and if you've never taken the time to be proud, do it now!). Would you ever trade that in and go back in time to change the circumstance to have taken that person's advice in the first place? Probably not. You know you weren't in a place then to take that advice, for whatever reason, even if it's eventually what you ended up doing. Your life lessons are yours. They hold unique gifts for you.

My point is: *We don't always know what's best for other people, even though we are convinced we do.*

But here's the more important point: When you find yourself on the obsessive side of trying to "help" someone, I can guarantee you're avoiding something in *your* life that needs your attention.

So what is it?

Is your own marriage a mess while you're trying to give oodles of relationship advice to your friend? Are you numbing your feelings by overeating while you tell your husband he drinks too much? Are you constantly up your son's ass for hanging out with losers while you hate your job?

In our minds, it seems easier to "fix" other people's lives instead of our own. It's less painful to focus on other people's problems. And if they get "better" because of your help, then you pat yourself on the back and feel validated. You feel important, smart, like a hero.

Do yourself and everyone else a favor: Give people a little credit. Remember it's *their* life, not yours. What you think about their decisions is all about you and really has nothing to do with them.

When you don't deal with your own issues, you're doing yourself a disservice and causing more suffering in your life. When you don't mention those pink elephants in the room and continue to act like things are "fine," you're not doing yourself any good. Well, guess what? The pink elephants don't magically disappear on their own, no matter how much we shove our noses in other people's business. How much "great" advice to others are you going to shell out before you deal with your own shit? Are you going to wait until it's so bad it's a red-alarm emergency?

I see this all the time and have done it in my own life. You know in your heart the things that you're not dealing with. I'm here to remind you those things are not going to get better if you ignore them. And they're not going to get better if you put all your energy into helping others. The problems stick around and fester like yesterday's garbage. The pile will keep getting bigger and bigger and you keep wondering who is going to take the trash out.

If this is you, take a break. Every time you feel the need to open your mouth and tell someone else what to do, turn your attention inward instead and think about what needs attention in *your* life. In case you forgot, you're important, too.

Give love and attention to your own shit. Remember the metaphor I gave you in Chapter 12 about taking on other people's piles of shit? You don't have to take it when they offer it to you (in the form of their judgments of you), *and* you don't have to willingly take it, either (in the form of you judging their actions).

CHAPTER 26

LIVING YOUR PASSIONS
= Living a Kick-Ass Life

We all have one thing that we really want to do—that thing that's rolled around in our head for a while that seems really fun and exciting. And I'll bet all of Oprah's money that you have *at least* one excuse as to why you haven't/can't/won't do it. And that the reason you haven't done it is because you let the excuse win.

I wrote about this in Chapter 2, so you already know about comfort zones, and in this chapter I want to emphasize the reasons *why* going after that thing you want to do is so important in living your kick-ass life. So here they are:

1. **You gain self-confidence and courage.** This one is pretty obvious. When you do that big thing you want to do, a spark starts inside of you. You find out that doing it wasn't as scary as the story you made it out to be. There are several layers to self-confidence and courage, and one of them is the notion of just *taking action*. Even if "your thing" turns out to be not as fun and exciting as you wanted it to be, at least you can look back on it and know that you actually *did* it.

2. **You meet lots of different people.** Say that thing you want to do is write a book, which is a dream for many. Once you go for it, you can join writing groups, go to author conferences, participate in National Novel Writing Month, and meet other people with the same dream or who are in the industry and can envision your dream. No matter what it is you want to do, there are loads of people just like you itching to do the same thing and loads of people that can help you achieve it.

3. **You'll have fewer regrets on your deathbed.** I just can't *imagine* what it must feel like to be at death's door and wish you would have opened that business, or started that hobby, or whatever is on your list. *Really* think about this one and what you want to be glad that you tried. It's not about accomplishing and fully succeeding at the thing you want to do, it's just about trying.

4. **You'll inspire others.** I can guarantee if you get out there and do it, you will hear over and over again, "You've inspired me to do _____!" The ripple effect can be enormous—one that you may never know the magnitude of. People will watch your example and see that if you can do it, they can, too. And better yet, if you reveal that you were scared before you did it but took action anyway, you'll inspire them even more.

5. **You'll have a positive thing to focus on.** Everyone needs a distraction from negative crap happening in their lives. There might come a day when you get to choose between drama and dreams. What would you choose?

6. **You'll just generally feel good.** And that's just epic. *You* feeling good is really why you want to do that thing in the first place. You want it because when you think about it, it makes you excited and happy, right? And that feels good. And when you feel good you pass that on to others and are just a generally healthier person emotionally (and probably physically, too!).

CHAPTER 27

LET GO
of Resentments

Have you ever heard the saying, "Holding onto resentments is like setting yourself on fire and hoping the other person chokes on your smoke?"

It's interesting to me when I hear someone say, "I like to hold a grudge" or "I just can't let it go."

I always ask, *"What the hell are you getting out of holding onto this?"*

(It's a rhetorical question.)

Are you thinking you're punishing this person you're holding the grudge against? Keeping them in your "resentment prison"? There is nothing to be gained from holding onto a grudge except anger, bitterness, hatred, and negativity—all dark, heavy emotions and energies. (And all things no one really wants to be around. Good luck making friends, sister.)

Do you do it because you think it makes you look tough? Because if you really stop and think about it, staying mad at someone and being unforgiving doesn't mean you're tough and unbreakable. It just means you're still pissed, and the only person suffering is you. If you enjoy that, then knock yourself out.

So why do it then?

Wait . . . would you like to tell me *your* story—along the lines of, "If she only knew what so-and-so did to me"?

Well, I don't give a shit what so-and-so did to you, or your momma. Letting go of resentment says absolutely nothing about what they did. It doesn't mean you think it's okay. It doesn't even mean you have to let them in your life anymore.

Letting go of resentment only means that you love yourself enough to let it all go.

And if you say there is no way you can let it go, I have to ask . . .

Why not?

What do you think will happen if you do? As you imagine, remember two important themes of this book:

1. Your worst-case fear story is probably not going to happen.
2. You can't control other people.

Just imagine what your life would be like without this resentment. After all, you don't have a time machine. You can't go back and force them to make a different choice. You can't even make them feel sorry for what he or she did. You can't make him or her ask you for forgiveness.

But, you *can* give yourself the freedom of ceasing to resent them for a decision *they* made. When you do this, you are moving on. Shedding old skin. Becoming a new, bigger, more powerful you.

Think about someone you're still mad at—I know there's *someone*. I'm sure when you think about her, you think about what happened and what she did. Now I'd like you to just think about what it would be like if you weren't mad anymore. I'm by no means saying you need to make up with this person, or even forgive her just yet . . . just think about what it would be like if you did not have feelings of anger and resentment towards her.

What would change inside of you?

Remember, this has nothing to do with her, but everything to do with you. Your resentment is yours. You created it, and you have the power to let it go.

This is one of the biggest gifts you can give yourself, not to mention others. Because when you let go of resentments, when you give yourself the gift of peace, you are essentially giving back to the people around you.

I found a journal of mine recently. I had been in a relationship with someone for about nine months after my ex-husband and I had split. I was a mess. (Back-to-back bad relationships will do that to a girl.)

In the journal I had written, *"What happened to me? People used to describe me as 'magnetic.' Where did I lose that girl? I want her back."*

What had happened is that I was holding onto resentments and anger toward that guy and my ex-husband. I was letting the actions of men determine me. I realized I had no control of them, or their actions—now or in the past.

So I let it go.

And I can tell you with absolutely no BS that that was a major shift in my life. I was taking a stand for my happiness, my freedom, and my life.

Resentment is heavy. So is anger and bitterness. Would you rather carry a light and peaceful load, or a heavy one? It's your choice. Before you decide, let me remind you that the person at the root of your negative thoughts and feelings really doesn't give a shit which load you're carrying.

CHAPTER 28

BE A LEGEND
in Your Own Mind

I remember the first time I heard the phrase, "Be a Legend in Your Own Mind." I thought to myself, *"Do I do this? Do I act like I'm a legend in my own mind?"*

And my true self answered: I certainly hope so.

And I enthusiastically hope you do the same.

It's not about being vain or conceited. It's about believing you are fucking awesome, because if *you* don't believe it, how are you going to get that awesome life you dream about? Because at the end of the day, it's all about what you believe. And the most important part is what you believe to be true about yourself.

How well do you treat yourself, in thoughts *and* in actions?

Because if you think you can't, you won't. If you think you're destined for failure, you'll fail. Not to mention, you'll be miserable in the meantime. And I don't know about you, but I think that seriously sucks.

So how do you think of yourself as a legend? Well, it's a very specific solution, one with many steps, long meditations, a strict diet, daily affirmations, and—

record scratching

No, it is actually simple: Make the decision. Here's some help:

1. Start by liking yourself. Say it out loud, say it in the mirror, say it to your dog.
2. Notice your inner critic. Just notice. After you notice, start remembering that it *is* your inner critic and doesn't have to be your truth (see Chapter 21).
3. Remember, you have bad days because you're human and we all do. Accept it and move forward.
4. Start over at number one and repeat.

Along with being a legend is living like one. What about the people you keep in your life? What about how you take care (or don't take care) of yourself? What about what you say out loud about yourself in front of others?

People are watching. And listening. And taking mental notes.

If you treat yourself like shit, others will, too. Maybe not every single person in the same way, but as a whole, they will. And if you're treated like shit, it will reiterate what kind of person you think you are, and you'll continue to treat yourself like shit because you think that's what you're worth. And then you're unconsciously looking for evidence of you being shitty, and you'll end up finding it. The people that you're around are treating you badly, and there's your evidence.

And that, my friend, is a bunch of . . . well, shit. It's a vicious cycle. One that will keep circling unless you change it.

You are priceless. I don't care who you are, what you've done, or what you currently think about yourself, you're legendary, just as you are.

You are the one thing you have 100 percent control over.

- *You* decide how you talk to yourself.
- *You* decide how you treat your body.
- *You* decide the people you let into your life.
- *You* decide what or who influences you.
- *You* decide what's important to you and if you honor that or not.

What decisions are you making on a regular basis that pertain to the above statements I just made?

You set the bar for how others should treat you. *You* allow people in your life, and *you* allow them to treat you a certain way. If you don't like it, ask them to change. If they won't, change how much you see them. It's that simple. I don't care if it's your mother, your twin sister, or your boss. You put up with what you put up with.

So . . . what are you tolerating that prevents you from feeling like a legend? Again, it's not about acting arrogant or conceited. It's about living your life in a way that reflects and reinforces how amazing you are, both in how you treat yourself and how you allow others to treat you.

CHAPTER 29

QUIT
Bitching and Moaning

Complaining is one of those universal things that people do to bond. Have you ever stood in an incredibly long line at the grocery store, exchanged frustrated looks with the person next to you, and one of you chimes in, "Would it be too hard for them to open a new line?" And you're suddenly BFFs. It's how we break the ice, bond, and ask for help.

But the truth is, more often than not, complaining accomplishes nothing.

Let me back up for a minute and give you a (brief) pass.

I do believe there is *some* good that can come out of conscious complaining, clearing, or venting. It's perfectly fine and dandy to say out loud the thing or circumstance you don't like. In fact, I believe if we totally avoid complaining and act like everything is peachy, we push our feelings down—and more harm can eventually come from that bad habit. The bottom line: Complaining can serve you as long as you have the intent to vent, *then shift and focus on the solution.*

Many people actually solve their own problems by saying them out loud. Some of my clients are this way. They get on the phone and announce: "I need to just talk about this for a few minutes—bear with me," and they spew it all out, and then end by saying, "I know what I need to do here is . . . " (And clearly, my brilliant work is done).

But here's where you might be shooting yourself in the foot: If you talk, talk, talk about how you don't like this or that, or how you wish blah, blah, blah, but take little or absolutely no action to change, then the excuse of, "Oh, but I can't change it," is—with all due respect—complete bullshit.

My dear friend and colleague, Amy Smith, always says: Don't complain about anything you're not willing to take action on.

So what are you willing to take action on?

First, try *asking* for what you want to change. Get clear on it before you talk to someone about it because sometimes we're not even sure what we want to change. If it is a person who is doing something you don't like, politely and respectfully tell that person how you feel and ask to come to some compromise so you can both be happy. Maybe this person wants to change the situation, too. You won't know unless you ask. Whether it's something about your job, or it's your neighbor's loud dog, just ask. If you don't ask, and you're focusing on what you don't like and complaining about it all the time, you're going to notice nothing but *that*. Nothing's going to change if you don't take action.

Plus, if you wait and wait, tension builds. When you've finally reached your breaking point and decide to discuss it with the person, most likely you're not going to be coming from a place of kindness and willingness to compromise. You'll be coming from a place of "you're-an-asshole-and-you-need-to-change-before-I-punch-you-in-the-throat." Not exactly conducive for a healthy discussion.

And if you really, truly can't change it—if it really, truly is all in the hands of someone else—*quit complaining about it!!* Let it go, for the love of God. I mean, how do you feel when you complain about it? Good? Empowered? Do you feel like your best self? Or is it a case of you feel good for the minute you say it out loud and then back to feeling like crap about it?

Complaining uses your precious energy and drives others away from you. Instead of expending that energy on negative things, spend it in positive ways. Fix problems. Love yourself and others.

But mainly, stop complaining!

CHAPTER 30

FORGIVE
Yourself

You already know how important it is to love yourself (see Chapter 19). The gospel truth here is you cannot truly love yourself if you are still beating yourself up for things you did in the past. The things you still mull over in your head could vary greatly. Maybe you had (or are having) an affair. Maybe you abused your body somehow, or maybe you were promiscuous as a teen, or you had an abortion, or maybe you just made some really terrible decisions somewhere along the line (P.S. *everyone* has).

It intrigues me that it's easier for people to forgive other people for hurting them than it is for them to forgive themselves for things they've done. It fascinates me how women will tell me they have confidence and self-love, yet when I ask them if they're forgiven themselves for all the mistakes they've made in the past I can almost see a ghost cross in front of their face. Then they reveal one or two things they've been dragging around.

I truly believe that by not forgiving ourselves we are participating in self-hate, which is the fastest way to living an unfulfilled, unhappy, and unkick-ass life. Not forgiving yourself is like that damn fly that will not leave you alone while you're trying to enjoy that summer BBQ. You keep swatting it away and go on enjoying yourself, but that pesky thing is relentless and just keeps showing up uninvited.

So, let's take a step back and look at whatever it was that you did that you can't seem to forgive yourself for.

Try your best to remember what your true intentions were at that time. Let's say you cheated on a partner. What were you actually looking for when you committed the act? If I had to guess, you were looking for comfort, validation, connection, and love. And at that time, your truest intention was to take care of yourself and get those feelings in the fastest way you knew how. Was the action the best way to get those feelings? Maybe not. But my point is that you were looking for basic, human, instinctual loving feelings. A way to take care of yourself the best way you knew how at that time.

When you look at it from this perspective, can you still hate yourself for your attempt to fulfill basic self-care?

Remember, you are human. By forgiving yourself, you're not saying it's okay to repeat the same mistakes. You're not saying it's okay for your children to do the same things. It doesn't mean anything except: **You love yourself enough to admit that you are a mortal human being who did the best you could with the tools you had at that time.**

Sometimes in the "human-ness" of us all, there is some "human-mess." We all have it. We all cope the best way we know how, at that time, with the tools we have. Learn from it and move on.

We all make mistakes, even disasters sometimes. Yet no one is benefitting from you holding on to this, certainly not you. What is the price you are paying for holding onto this? Are you more stressed, less ambitious, less happy, less fulfilled? It's not worth it!

Even if you know it's the right thing to do, forgiving yourself can be difficult. To start, make a list of all the things you beat yourself up for. Whether you come down on yourself on a regular basis or every once in a while, write it all out. Yes, it might be painful to see it in front of you, but do it anyway. Sometimes getting it all out of you helps the past lose its power over you. It's as if you've purged it—your past just becomes words on a page and isn't as horrific and gargantuan as you've made it out to be.

Even if you know it's the right thing to do, forgiving yourself can be difficult.

Then make the decision to forgive yourself. If this is too hard at this point, try making peace with the situation. "It" happened. No more soul beatings. And if you still think it's too hard to forgive yourself, think about the alternative—which is continuing to hold resentments against yourself. Say it again: At the time you did whatever it was that you did, you did the best you could with the tools you had at that time. Otherwise, you would have done things differently.

Think about this: If it were your child, or your partner, or your best friend and they did what you did, then truly felt remorseful and asked for forgiveness, and you truly believed that they did the best they could at that time they made the mistake, would you forgive them? Or would you tell them, "Nah, you still need to suffer."

I don't think so.

Imagine what would happen if you allowed *yourself* to move away from past mistakes in the same way.

You deserve forgiveness. You deserve peace. You deserve to let go of what's holding you back.

CHAPTER 31

HONOR
Your Soul's Uniqueness

There's a big, nasty word out there and I'd like to talk to you about it: conformity.

I believe our culture does not make it easy for us to embrace who we truly are. And if you're a woman (I may be biased), it's even harder. We're told how we should look, act, and talk; what is "beautiful;" how to "succeed." Hell, even the definition of success is given to us.

In this way, a "box" of conformity is created. It looks pretty much the same for everyone. And the reason many of us get in this box is because we want to be accepted and this seems like the easiest way to do it. Usually this happens right around middle school for many of us. We adopt the opinions, beliefs, preferences, and hobbies of others. And then we grow up and these conforming habits stick with us. And we can't figure out why we're unhappy.

Did you get in the box at some point in your life? If you did, you had a lot of company.

I finally got out around thirty-one years old. At that point, I defined my own success, happiness, fulfillment, values, future, and everything else. And it's my biggest wish for everyone to do the same.

If you don't define yourself, it's easy to go through life like a sheep, following the crowd, not knowing what you like, what you want, and who you truly are. Not knowing what it is that makes you shine.

That is a tragedy.

I meet people all the time who don't feel like there is anything special about them. They spend so much time, money, and energy trying to be like someone else. Someone they think has a fantastic life. Someone they think has it easier than they do. Even if you're not doing that right now, maybe you remember a time when you did.

What's that like, trying to be like someone else? Comfortable? Easy? I didn't think so.

Forgive me for sounding so cliché here, but I truly believe that if everyone realized the power of their special uniqueness, the entire world would be a better place.

If you realized that there is absolutely no one like you, what would you embrace? What would you stop apologizing for? Would you know there is nothing "wrong" with you? That you are not broken, that you don't need to be more like so-and-so, that you can say "no" to people and things you don't like, and say "yes" more often to the things that light you up? That you are absolutely 100 percent perfect exactly the way you are? Imagine the power within you!

I've written this little manifesto for you on how to embrace your soul's uniqueness. It goes like this:

Love yourself. With all your heart and with all your soul. There might be days when this is hard, and that's okay. Just pick up where you left off the next day. Our time here on this beautiful earth is short; do with it what you want. Stop before you do things you think you should do just because other people are doing them, or telling you that you should. What's important to you should be important to you, period. Don't compromise your feelings and values. And if you do, promise not to tell yourself, "I told you so." Listen to your heart and soul. It often speaks to you in whispers. I promise if you follow it, you won't be disappointed in the end.

Love yourself. With all your heart and with all your soul.

Who you are is who you are. There is not a single soul on earth or beyond who is exactly like you. Instead of running from that knowledge, try grasping it. It's perfectly okay to be you, and if people don't like it, trust me when I tell you (again) it really has nothing to do with you, but rather their own opinions and insecurities.

Try your best not to be careless with other people's hearts. Yours will get broken at least once in your life. We all have scars on our hearts; it's what makes us human and beautiful and unique. Forgive yourself often. Daily, if you must. You'll spend much of your life being too hard on yourself, so try to catch it quickly and give yourself a break. You don't have to do it all. And you especially don't have to do it all at the same time. If you think that everyone else is doing it, trust me, they aren't. Everyone struggles. No matter how good they look on the outside, and no matter how much they brag about it. And those girls and women that make it look so easy, they struggle, too. And hurt. And have fears just like you and me.

And last, embrace other women. Be compassionate. The "mean girls" are hurting, too, so try not to hate them. On that same note, no one is worth hating. No person, no institution, no idea. Kindness and love will get you everywhere your dreams want, especially when you love and are kind to yourself first.

I invite you to just plant a seed in your mind that says, "I am me, and I am amazing, kick-ass, courageous, and lovable exactly how I am."

Just as you are.

CHAPTER 32

START
Something!

I truly believe we are all creative beings. I also believe we are all passionate about something.

Those two things together are like fire and gasoline. Put them together and you got yourself a raging inferno. In a good way, of course.

If you don't care about your inherent passion or your God-given creative strengths, skip this chapter.

Ladies and gentlemen:

Life is for living.

Scratch that.

Life is for grabbing by the throat and through gritted teeth saying, "This life is mine. I will live it with all I've got. I won't take crap from anyone, won't play small, or safe. I will admit that I'm a kick-ass. I can break *through* after a break*down*. I can get up after I fall down on my face."

(Okay, so that might have been a little dramatic, but I think you get the gist.)

A big part of living a kick-ass life and having those inspiring moments like the one I just mentioned is to tap into your natural creativity. Bringing it to light regularly is what will fuel you and help you become your most kick-ass self.

Let me dispel a common myth. Creativity isn't a special gift only given to a lucky few. I truly believe we are all born with creativity, and somewhere along the line in life we forget about it, or it escapes us. Here are some ways to get it back:

- **Practice gratitude.** See Chapter 44 for more on this topic. Practicing gratitude opens up good feelings and promotes self-love. When we're grateful we tend to attract and manifest not only what we truly want, but what dormant creativity might be there waiting to be sparked, too.
- **Read, watch movies, go to plays, etc.** The key is to digest a hodgepodge of themes. Adventure, humor, drama—whatever. The stories invite your brain to bounce around a bit and not stick to one idea. In addition, if music is your thing, go with that. If I'm in a creative funk, I put on disco, then switch to classic rock, then some '80s—and all the stress and funkiness goes away and I'm back to whatever creative project I want.
- **Join or start a book or writing club.** Or any kind of creativity group for that matter. Being around "your tribe" will ignite your creative juices and lift your spirits.
- **Meditate and do yoga.** This is about being still. Sometimes our minds get so overloaded, it's as if we have 2,974 browser windows open at the same time and can't get and keep a single thought together. Meditation and yoga can help calm all of that down and let you reboot your mind, and then kick-start your creativity.
- **Be a kid again.** Children have unlimited amounts of imagination and creativity that just ooze out of them. When was the last time you colored in a coloring book, or played with Legos or Play-Doh? Here's the thing with this one: Make sure you're tapping into *your*

inner child, not someone else's version. To be honest, playing with Play-Doh makes me want to gouge my eyes out. So for me to do this in order to spark creativity is futile because I never liked doing it as a kid. Now, running through the sprinklers is an entirely different story. Do what *you* want to do that's childlike and fun.

Also, try not to get the ideas of "creating" and "being creative" confused. I for one used to think being creative meant being an artist or a playwright, or maybe even preschoolers proudly holding up their finger paintings.

Creating isn't only that. It can simply mean expressing who you are as an individual. What might be creative for you is actually creating yourself. Creating the person you want to be, the person you were meant to be. (And know that by doing that, you're actually creating your own revolution of sorts—by standing up for who you are and not who you think you should be.)

Your creating, your revolution, your *something* is fuel for your life.

Whatever is there is your own personal revolution; your own inferno. Go now.

CHAPTER 33

MOVE OUT
of Victimhood

Have you ever been the guest of honor at your own pity party? I thought so. While it's completely normal, and I think healthy, to feel bad about a situation you're in, to feel sad, or frustrated, or whatever feelings you need to feel about your current circumstances, if you're setting up residency there . . . you might be living in victimhood.

This type of person is committed to the story that she is destined to live "this crappy, hard life." She can never seem to catch a break and it's always someone else's fault. She thinks everyone is out to get her, as if people put in extra effort to make her life suck. She thinks she got dealt a bad hand from the start and can just never seem to get ahead of the game.

If you just read your own biography, keep reading. This chapter is for you, my dear.

Victimhood is the killer of your highest self. You are literally handing out your power to other people. Handing out your power to circumstances. Handing out your power to the atmosphere—pretty much handing it out to nothing. Giving it away. Flushing it down the toilet.

Things happen. Shit happens. We all have everything from unpleasant to downright catastrophic things happen in our lives.

Living in victimhood wears on you (not to mention the people around you), feeds on itself, and will give you more of the same. The more you complain and are convinced you're destined for failure, the more of that you will get. And even if your life looks different to other people, even if you're on the upswing, you'll still feel like your life sucks.

It's like a gum wrapper on the floor of the Sistine Chapel. Most people would think nothing of it, because they are focused on the beauty and awe of what is around them.

But then there's that person who only sees the trash. He complains about it, tells everyone there about it, misses the beauty of the Sistine Chapel, and doesn't remember anything about the art. He only remembers the gum wrapper. If this person had shifted his perspective, simply moved his eyes away from the wrapper and looked up and around him, he would see a completely different space. One that would quite possibly leave him breathless and awestruck.

My point is that you always have a choice when it comes to your perspective. Gum wrapper or Sistine Chapel? Endless possibilities in your life, or a victim of your circumstances?

Victimhood is suffering that you are essentially putting on yourself. Ask yourself: *What am I getting out of being addicted to suffering?*

And here's another hard truth: People don't like to be around other people who act like victims. It's exhausting. It's sad. It's emotionally taxing. There's nothing fun or exciting or loving about it.

Honey, I'm sorry if you've had a hard life. But if you want it to stop, quit looking for everything else around you to change and start with yourself.

Here's how. You'll notice that a lot of these themes are starting to sound familiar. That's because they're true, and they're important.

1. **Reach your breaking point:** Get to a place where you're sick and tired of being sick and tired. If you're in denial about being in victimhood . . . I sincerely hope this is your wake-up call. Draw a line in the sand. Declare that you are *done*. Once you accept this is all up to you, that you have the key in your hand to get out of this prison, I hope to God you unlock the door and get out.

2. **Take responsibility for your life.** For starters, take responsibility for your thoughts. Remember your thoughts, not your circumstances, determine your feelings. Your thoughts are determining that you are feeling like a victim. How about instead of thinking, "I'm so devastated this happened to me," you flip it to, "I'm really upset this happened." Easy. Small tweak. It didn't happen *to* you, it just happened. I'm not asking you to move mountains with your thinking and start believing fluffy affirmations. Just start slow and progress from there.

3. **Ask yourself what you can do to move forward, even just a little.** It doesn't have to be leaps and bounds at first. Even if you just declare, "I will *not* be a victim anymore." Start with those three steps. Declare that your old victim story is now in your past.

Maybe some people are just born pessimists, chronic "downers," but I don't think so. If you feel that way, I want you to know that you can change. Read books like this one, join support groups, ask your doctor if you need meds for your depression or anxiety, change your diet—just don't use excuses or bullshit stories.

You deserve the best, my friend. Victimhood is *not* the best.

CHAPTER 34

You Are Always
WORTHY OF LOVE

You have probably been through some tough times in your life. For example: Say your ex or current partner has been unfaithful. Major betrayal, right? I know, because it's happened to me more than once. I was hurt, sad, scared, furious, ashamed, humiliated, and betrayed. No matter what's happened to you, those feelings are common reactions to a host of terrible life circumstances. At one point, I even referred to and described myself as "destroyed."

Yes, destroyed. By whom or what? My ex? The cheating? The other woman? The circumstance? I'm not even sure I knew. But it was easier for me to point my finger at him and say that he and what he did had destroyed me. It was a way for me to try to hurt him (didn't work). It was a way for me to stay a victim. It was a way for me to garner pity from others and get them on "my side."

Was it empowering? Not so much.

Did it help me move on? Nope.

Did it help me reaffirm that I still was and am, in fact, a great person? No, no, no.

Whether something "happened" to you, or you made a mistake yourself, remember: You're human. You have feelings that take a while to work through and sometimes they need to be worked through over and over again. You can't put an expiration date on them, or a deadline of when you want them to be done. But you also need to remember: Your circumstances surrounding your life, and the thoughts and feelings around them, don't define you. They may shape you, but they don't make you who you are.

Tell yourself this, and often: **You are worthy of love, acceptance, and connection no matter who you are, what you've done, or what you've been through.** You are not "damaged" or "destroyed." (If you truly think you are, jump to Chapter 52.) Your feelings may be hurt, you may have regrets, but *you* as a sacred being are a whole person and you are still unimaginably magnificent.

If you've ever had a conversation with yourself or someone else that sounds like this, I'm talking to you:

Well, if so-and-so wouldn't have done _____ *to me, I could be* _____.

I would do _____, *but I can't because I've been devastated by* _____.

No one is magic enough to give your feelings to you. *No one. You* determine them every second of every day. Your thoughts, your reactions to what other people do, your commitments to stories in your head, and your subsequent beliefs are what make your feelings. Not someone else's words or actions.

Ever.

Think for a minute about a time when someone had done something that hurt you. Are you angry? Hurt? Scared? It's perfectly fine to feel that way. *But if these feelings are causing you to feel negatively about yourself or to make decisions in your life that aren't serving you, there's work that needs to be done.*

Don't let lingering negative feelings about what happened to you in the past limit who you can be in the future.

Everyone has baggage. Everyone has a past. No matter what yours looks like, you are still a person whose dreams should be realized. A person who deserves to be loved. A person whose life purpose—whatever it is—is important to humankind. Don't let lingering negative feelings about what happened to you in the past limit who you can be in the future. Remind yourself that you're legendary. You're amazing. You're . . . kick-ass.

CHAPTER 35

PURSUING PERFECTION
Is the Race to Nowhere

I'll be honest, out of all fifty-two chapters of this entire book, this one is the hardest for me. The pursuit of perfection has been my poison apple for as long as I can remember. This is one of those "one-day-at-a-time" practices for me, and it might be the same for you as well. (I *can* say I've come a long, long way from where I used to be.)

If you're reading this book, chances are you want to become more self-aware, participate in your own self-growth and development, and just generally live a great life. And if you *really* want your life to kick ass, well, trust me when I tell you that you *must* work on letting go of perfection. I'm guessing you already know that. The thing is, I know it, too. My logical brain understands that perfection doesn't exist, and striving for it will turn up nothing but more anxiety, negative self-talk, and subsequent misery. But it's one of those things that can creep up as a default goal for many of us.

Where I see perfectionism hurting women is when they don't go after what they want in fear of not doing it perfectly. Fear, comparison, negative self-talk, and our culture's pressure on women today all add up to create the perfect storm. It's the "go big or go home" mentality. Black or white; perfect or not at all. Somewhere we crossed the line from the woman who is striving for excellence, a go-getter, and ambitious, to this perfectionist who's suffocating under all the pressure.

So, where is this line and how do you avoid crossing it?

The first step is to be okay with the fact this might be one of your areas of kryptonite. Hearing "Don't be a perfectionist!" and "Embrace imperfections!" is like asking someone who loves mac-n-cheese with cut-up hot dogs to prepare and serve a gourmet meal to ten people in an hour. It's anxiety-inducing and seemingly impossible.

Still, simply recognizing and admitting that this is hard for you is helpful. Yes, perfectionistic inner critics will go kicking and screaming, clawing their perfectly manicured nails. Tell yourself something like, "This might be really hard for me, but I love myself and am willing to try." Or, "Perfectionism is a big part of me, but it isn't serving me. I'm ready for change, day by day." The key here is kindness.

Second is to personify your inner perfectionist (this is also a great exercise for Chapter 21). Mine, of course, is perfect and wants nothing else but for me to be as well. I call her "Vicious Bitch." I see her and personify her looking like a mannequin. Nothing out of place, impossibly thin, accessorized, hairless in most places, and symbolically empty inside. Yours might be a character from a movie, a former boyfriend or girlfriend, or perhaps your mother. Try to create a character you can think of when you feel your perfectionism rearing its ugly head. The point of this exercise is to be able to separate your true self from this voice. Because I guarantee you, with every ounce of my being, your perfectionistic voice is not truly who you are.

Promise.

Third is to approach this inner perfectionist with . . . are you ready? Compassion. The thing is, this part of you is scared. It's so afraid of looking foolish, stupid, inadequate, not good enough, smart enough, fill-in-the-blank enough, her only way of avoiding that is to demand nothing but perfection. If you can peel back her layers and really look at her, I would bet you would not want to shun her, kick her ass, or tell her how wrong she is—you'd want to give her a hug, a break, and tell her it'll all be okay.

So here's the deal: When you find yourself holding back because of perfectionism, or talking shit to yourself about not being the absolute best, my challenge to you is to take a look at that part of you that really is hurting. Life's not always about kicking ass and taking names. There's plenty of (necessary) room for you to honor the parts of you that need your absolute love and attention in order to move past them and be a better version of yourself.

I'll leave you with some of my favorite quotes from some of my mentors and colleagues about perfectionism . . .

- *"Imperfections are not inadequacies; they are reminders that we're all in this together."* —Brené Brown
- *"Being imperfect is blissfully expansive. If I had it all figured out, growth wouldn't be necessary. And to me, growth is joyful . . . even when it's uncomfortable."* —Tanya Geisler
- *"Imperfection has taught me acceptance, which isn't easy for a right-brained perfectionist to do. I compartmentalize my imperfection, as in: I'll never be a perfect cook or perfect mother and don't try to be. I just want to be authentic and loving to my kiddos."* —Melissa Wardy
- *"I'm happily imperfect, with my life motto 'ancora imparo'—'I am still learning.' (It's on my door. In my parenting. And gives me permission to be real.) Guess it's kind of like a self-rendered hall pass to say, 'Hey, I'm doing the best I can.' In fact, if I had to write my own epitaph on my tombstone tomorrow it would be two words: 'She tried.'"* —Amy Jussel

- *"Imperfection gives me something in common with everyone else in the world."* —Ashley Folsom
- *"If I had it all figured out, what would I be doing here? Imperfection helps to give my life meaning and purpose. It creates twists and turns that keep the journey so interesting, I wouldn't want to reach my destination."* —Angela Lauria

CHAPTER 36

TAKE RESPONSIBILITY for Your Dysfunctional Relationship

This one is dear to my heart because it comes from my own real-life story. Years ago, I was a responsible party in creating a relationship that wasn't serving either of us. I wasn't being treated well, the relationship was going nowhere, and I stuck around for it. For years, I was committed to thinking:

"Eventually, he'll change. Then the relationship will be great."

In the meantime, I scrambled and hustled to be what I thought I needed to be in order for him to change. Smart, right?

The years passed. Nothing changed.

I was too scared to leave, to start over, and to be alone. To possibly spend my thirties alone was terrifying.

I was in love and addicted to a fantasy of this life that I longed for. And every day I woke up and hoped that would be the day my fantasy would come true. And guess what?

It didn't.

Once I stopped blaming him for my miserable life, then I started to see things more clearly and move on. I see this over and over again: people in relationships who wait around for their partner to change. How many people do you know who spend ample amounts of time bitching, complaining, wishing, and hoping for their partner to change and then, voilà! One day they do change! All the pushing, pleading, and complaining worked.

Zero.

Like I've said before: You are the only one that can control you, and *you* are the only one that can make you miserable.

If you're in a relationship where the other person treats you like crap, remember: You're the one who is sticking around for the crap, deep down knowing it isn't going to get better.

And perhaps you're sticking around because you're hanging onto the "if only . . ." notion. If only he would propose. If only he would get a job. If only he would stop cheating on me. If only he would stop drinking.

If you're in love with the notion of "if only," remember that it is an imaginary fantasy that isn't going to show up to give you the love and respect you truly deserve.

And ask yourself this: Are you really in love with your partner . . . or are you in love with the glimmers of hope, the "if onlys"? With the fantasy you've made up of how it *could* be? Are there two different stories going on here—the reality of what is happening in the relationship and then the fictional story you've made up? If it's the latter, take a look at the current reality in your relationship. If things keep going exactly how they are, is the story going to turn out how you want it? And if you think it is, how long are you willing to wait? Ten years? Forever?

This bears repeating over and over: You deserve love and respect. It needs to come from you first, so if you truly love and respect yourself, you wouldn't stay in a destructive, dysfunctional relationship. I know this; I was that girl in the relationship where, looking back, I didn't love and respect myself. I wanted to, but I didn't know how.

So, how do you?

1. **Be okay with the fact that you don't exactly know how to respect yourself.** You can spend years lost in a cycle and feeling like a victim to "not knowing how." Resolve to get off that merry-go-round.

2. **Take inventory of what you're tolerating in your relationship.** You've probably made the mental list 100,000 times in your mind, so now's your chance to organize it, write it down, and see it in black and white in front of your face. Is there emotional disconnect? Is there infidelity? Disrespect? List it all out.

3. **Decide that you are not going to tolerate anything but love and respect in your relationships.** If you're in a relationship that isn't serving you, where your partner is anything from disrespectful to abusive, please hear me when I tell you that it is highly unlikely that this person is going to change. Yes, there might be .005 percent who do, but these people go through years of therapy and help before they change. And many times, the relationships don't last through the changes. This is a hard truth to swallow, but a necessary one.

4. **Get professional help if you're committed to helping the relationship.** Couples counseling works and saves relationships. But, *both* parties need to be not only willing, but committed. If your partner is unwilling to get help in your relationship, I hate to say it . . . but that is an indicator that this person really *does* have issues that need to be helped (and he/she is afraid to face them), plus it's not a good sign of a healthy future for the relationship.

5. **Get to know yourself.** What do you want in life? What do you *not* want? What do you think of yourself? How do you want to change? Hopefully this book will help you get to know yourself a little more. (If you're still totally lost, see Chapter 51.)

And one more thing . . . if you're not ready to leave, you're not ready. Everyone has a different threshold for pain when it comes to difficult relationships. Some people can stick around for a whole heap of crap before they've had enough. *You* need to decide where you draw the line in the sand and cannot tolerate any more. My hope is that at the very least, this chapter will help you realize exactly what's going on, what you're putting up with, and what the future really looks like.

Because your future deserves to kick ass.

CHAPTER 37

Don't Let
COMPARISONS
Destroy You

Have you ever compared yourself to someone else? Never? Okay, robot: Skip to the next chapter.

If you're a human being, keep reading.

I'll bet if I asked you right now, you could name five people who you think are perfect—either people you know or don't know. They are beautiful, have the perfect house, perfect spouse, perfect life. You wish you could either be them, or have everything they have. You're convinced they have little to no pain in their perfect lives, and if only your life could be like theirs, everything would be, well . . . perfect.

My husband left me for another woman at exactly the same time Brad Pitt left Jennifer Aniston (not like I know that for sure—for all I know, she kicked his ass out). I saw her on the cover of a tabloid magazine and wondered how hard it must be to have to deal with that pain in front of the world. Practically on stage. I also wondered if it was easier for her than it was for me. After all, she had millions of dollars, a perfect body, perfect tan, perfect hair, and an awesome career.

But I realized, at the end of the day, she's still a human being, just like me. Just like you.

"Stuff," or money, or looks, or anything else doesn't make painful circumstances any less painful. And even if your perfect people don't look like they're suffering now, I spit-swear guarantee that they have had pain, suffering, insecurities, and fear just like you and me. If you see it any other way, it just means they just do a really good job of covering it up. Before you go comparing yourself to your perfect people, just remember that everyone suffers in their own way. Live the life you were given, for it was given to you for a reason. Pain and all.

There's a saying that goes, "If everyone threw all their problems in a pile for everyone else to see, we'd take our own back." I absolutely believe this to be true.

Here are some tools to help you when you find your thoughts serving up a steamy pile of comparison crap:

* The first is what I like to call "labeling." We think, "If she is prettier than me, then I'm ugly." We label ourselves based on what we think about someone else. Instead, what if it just . . . was? For instance, shift it to, "If she is prettier than me, then she is just prettier than me." *It doesn't mean anything.* My hope is that instead of immediately trying to jump all the way from disempowering thoughts to positive, affirming ones (which I know can be really difficult), you can start by moving from a place of disempowerment to a middle ground of neutrality. Your first goal can be to shift your thoughts from, "She's prettier than me" to, "Wow, she's really pretty." The end. Empowerment can come later when you're feeling safe in neutrality.
* The second tool here is gratitude. I talk about this more in Chapter 44 and this is often my go-to tool. When you find yourself falling down the rabbit hole of comparing, stop and immediately list as

many things you can think of that you are grateful for. It's really hard to keep comparing, beating yourself up, and wishing you were different when your thoughts are inundated by things you love and are grateful for.

- Dovetailing off the last one is celebrating your own accomplishments. Have you stopped lately to be proud of what *you've* accomplished lately? Or ever? If this is a void in your life, it will be easier for you to fall prey to the comparison trap.

- Don't hate, appreciate. Not long ago I was in a bistro with a friend and we were asking the girl behind the counter about the food there. This girl was beautiful. With not very much make-up on, if any, she had gorgeous skin, a sprinkle of freckles, and bright eyes. I interrupted her spiel about sandwiches and said, "You are gorgeous!" I could have let my mind wander to how much older I was than she, that I have crows' feet and she didn't . . . but instead, I stood back and appreciated her beauty and told her so. All of us can appreciate beautiful jewelry, a sunset, or a piece of art. What if we appreciated another woman's beauty, or congratulated her for her success, or celebrated her instead of finding a way to bring ourselves down.

Comparison relates to perfectionism (see Chapter 35). The truth is there will always be someone who is stronger, prettier, richer, etc. There will always be someone to compare yourself to. Catch your comparison thinking before it spins out of control into disempowering, negative self-thoughts. Instead, separate yourself from what you're looking at, and appreciate the other thing for what it is.

CHAPTER 38

A C+ Day Can
CHANGE YOUR LIFE

Several years ago, I attended a weekend training session to be a life coach. My wedding was the very next weekend, so, needless to say, I was not mentally present in my training weekend; I was extremely conflicted. As much as I tried to focus on what was in front of me, my mind kept wandering to my upcoming wedding.

At a break, I pulled aside one of the leaders and told her my situation. She paused and said, "What if you just gave yourself permission to have a C+ weekend? To not do A+ work and just be where you are?"

But the truth was, the other way wasn't working, either. I couldn't concentrate, and beating myself up about it wasn't helping. So I begrudgingly decided to take her advice, try giving myself a break and let go of being an honor student, at least just for the rest of the day.

And the funniest thing happened.

I ended up relaxing and absorbing more than I thought I would.

The thing is, none of us can fire on all cylinders 100 percent of the time. No one is the Terminator. We all have hard days, distractions, pressures of life, etc. And having a C+ day is all about perspective. It's also about having the attitude of "good enough."

Ahhhh . . . good enough.

So, what *is* good enough to you? How good do you think you have to be at something? At some point you (or you adopted it from someone else) made a mental list of criteria that is the definition of your "good enough." The problem is that many people confuse "good enough" with "perfect." Because most people's "good enough" is never actually enough for them. And "perfect" is something no one ever can attain. So from that perspective, it's a lose/lose situation.

I'm not saying throw your hands in the air with a "fuck it" mentality, going against what you believe in and what's fundamentally comfortable for you. But keep in mind, a C+ day for a perfectionist is probably an A day in realistic standards. Determine objectively what is standard A excellence, and then where *you* cross the line into unrealistic perfectionism. If you start to think about this, you'll start to notice your triggers and be able to catch negative spirals more quickly.

So, how do you practice being "good enough"?

It starts with making a decision. When some people hear this, they want to punch me in the face—and no, it's not as easy as just waking up one day, deciding, and it's a done deal. First try *accepting* that you are absolutely the only person who can decide you are "good enough." It probably feels powerful and scary at the same time.

If you keep falling into perfectionism, try redefining what perfect is. For example, when I was training for my first triathlon, I was terrified of the open water swim. I'm not a great swimmer, plus I had a fear of open water (I mean, what's *in* there? Jaws? How deep is it, 100 miles? Blechhh). I began placing time goals on myself, and feeling scared, pressured, competitive, and needing to not only do this triathlon, but also do it perfectly. Which wasn't fun at all.

Finally, knowing I couldn't do it perfectly, I changed my goal to just finishing the damn race. Try my best not to drown or get eaten by a sea creature, not worry about my time and where I was placing, and just finish. And trust me when I tell you it was waaay more fun that way. It was my C+, good-enough race.

The bare minimum in feeling good enough is to practice self-kindness. It might mean repeating a mantra that is simply, "It's good enough" when it comes to projects, actions, and decisions, and saying, "I'm good enough" over and over again to yourself. Most times, it's a one-day-at-a-time practice. Sometimes one-hour-at-a-time. The bottom line is to give yourself a break and keep on truckin'.

The bare minimum in feeling good enough is to practice self-kindness.

One exercise I give to my clients is to create a to-do list that their inner perfectionist, or inner critic, would make. Don't hold back. If your inner critic thinks you need to go back and finish your master's this year even though you just had a baby, put it on there. Or maybe on the list is that you need to be successful and making six-figures this year, even though last year you made 30k. Then, make another to-do list that is *realistic*. That's your "good enough" list. While I'm all for the law of attraction and manifesting what you want . . . *it needs to feel good, easy, and peaceful* energetically speaking.

Your goals, aspirations, and to-do list shouldn't feel stressful or destined for failure. If it does, your inner critic is making that to-do list. Instead, you want to feel motivated, powerful, and inspired. Your "good enough" list can help you find those feelings. Take back your power and make your own.

CHAPTER 39

Don't
DEFINE YOURSELF
Through Others

This chapter isn't about the labeling I explained a couple chapters ago. What this chapter talks about is defining yourself by esteeming yourself through others. Getting validation through external sources is one of the common reasons women come to me for help. They can't seem to get off the ride of only feeling confident, happy, and worthy because someone told them to feel that way.

I used to be that way, too, and I'll admit it—sometimes I slip back.

Let me start by saying it's really, really great to be affirmed. And there is nothing wrong with having words of affirmation from others be something that's important to you. When it becomes a problem is when it's the *only* time you feel good. When it becomes one of your basic needs.

If this happens chronically, you're basically handing over your personal power to other people. You've become a puppet on a string, and most of the time, the puppeteer doesn't even know he or she has this job.

Not sure if this is you? Here's a quick list of things to look for:

- You fish for compliments.
- You get upset if someone doesn't notice your new haircut, outfit, or actions you've done.
- You try to spend time with people who stroke your ego.
- You might be highly competitive.
- You put a lot of emphasis on how many Facebook friends you have, comments, followers, etc.

If this is you, somewhere along the line you've made other people's opinions more important than your own. Or perhaps you haven't even shaped your opinions of yourself yet. Just remember, you were given your own mind so you wouldn't just digest and accept opinions from others. You were given a mind to create your own definition of yourself and have your own opinions about everything.

This behavior may have come from your childhood, a former or current relationship, your peers, or really anything in your life. The point here isn't to place blame on whom or what shaped this behavior, but for you to know this is a *learned* behavior that can be shifted. There is no reason you have to get to the end of your life and wonder, "What just happened . . . who was I?" Also, by looking at where the need for external validation behavior might have come from, you can see that it came from something outside of you, perhaps someone else's opinion—it was never yours in the first place.

And here's the ass-kicker with this topic: Most of the time when people realize they are defining themselves through others and then want to change, they get stuck because they have no idea what they really want, who they really are deep inside themselves, or even what they really believe in. (Chapters 4 on values and 13 on nonnegotiables may have been especially difficult.)

I have yet to meet a person, myself included, who was able to recognize that they define themselves through others and then are easily able to go in the other direction: not to give a rat's ass about what other people think and suddenly validate themselves. With a challenge like learning to validate and define yourself, it's helpful to take small steps. A great place to start is an exercise I've borrowed from the brilliant mind of Martha Beck called, "Defining Your Everybody Committee." First step in the exercise is to fill in the following blanks:

- "Everyone thinks I'm _____."
- "Everyone wants me to _____."
- "Everyone's always telling me _____."

After you've answered these questions, ask yourself who *exactly* are the people you're referring to here. Not the people you *think* expect you to be a certain way, but those you *know* feel that way because they've told you so. Typically, people have one person on this list and no more than six. And sometimes, it's *no one*. That's a real wake-up call that you need to define yourself how *you* think you should. Yet somehow, somewhere, we've managed to create an idea that one person's opinion is the same opinion of an entire global population.

Kinda crazy, right?

Chances are, you are either directly or indirectly seeking validation from the people on your short (or nonexistent) list of "everybody." Simply by noticing this and being aware, you can begin to move away from getting your validation solely from others. Remember, you choose whom you surround yourself with (see Chapter 45). If necessary, you can appoint a new committee.

I also believe many of the behaviors we do to feel good (some of which become bad habits), we do as a means to feel safe. It might feel "unsafe" to try to feel good about yourself through your own definition, since you have little experience trusting your instincts and knowing what *you* want out of life. Looking outside of yourself for love, validation, and esteem is a very unsafe and unstable means of feeling good. You can provide yourself all the love and stability you need, on your own terms.

CHAPTER 40

BOLDLY STAND UP
for What You Believe, Even If It's Unpopular

What really pisses you off?

Everyone has something, probably a whole list of things, ranging from little irritations to things that reduce them to "I'm a'-gonna kick that person's ass" pissed off.

What is that thing you want to get up on your soapbox and tell everyone and their mother about? That thing you feel you need to convince everyone you are right about? Got it?

Okay, that's your "thing." The thing you truly believe in. You feel it in your bones; it runs through your blood; it's *inside* of you. It might be how you feel about the environment, animal rights, political topics, feminism, or the existence of unicorns—*anything* that is important to you.

There are very few things every person on the planet can agree on. Even if you think your issue is something everyone is on board with, such as agreeing no one should go hungry, you'd be surprised . . . I'm pretty sure there's some asshole out there who feels differently.

Yet, you might be a people pleaser (see Chapter 7), and in standing up for what you believe in you might piss some people off, which can make you very uncomfortable. Or worse, someone might not like you (gasp!).

This topic was put to the test for me while writing this book. Just like you, I'm human, and I still have that inner critic that creeps in and talks shit to me about pissing people off while I stand up for what I believe in. With all the practice and work I've done over the years, I'm really good at managing that voice, but while writing, I had some fearful thoughts of, *"This book is really going to piss some people off."*

My heart said most people would like it; love it, even. But underneath all my courage and confidence, I had little moments of creative freak-out. The fear of pissing people off on such a grand scale was new for me. It's taken my inner critic to a whole new level.

I can't please everyone; none of us can. What I know to be true is when we piss people off, we've struck a chord with them. And so we can lean into the freak-outs, work on our thoughts, or call a friend/colleague, and eventually the freak-out passes.

When you stand up for what's inside of you, you're living your life's purpose and honoring your values. You're more likely to be fulfilled and happy and live a kick-ass life. Be an example to your kids, to other women around you, to anyone who's listening. They might not agree, and they might even judge or criticize you for it. In fact, I can almost guarantee someone will. If you care so much about what other people think or say, sister, let me tell you—no, let me beg you—*let that go*. There will always be critics. Always.

Finding the courage and personal fortitude to stand up for your beliefs takes practice, just like anything else. I remember when I got my first "you are the stupidest person ever for thinking this/writing about it" comment on my blog. I was devastated. Cried about it. Thought about editing the post. But I stayed strong because I believed what I wrote. And the next time I got a comment like that, I handled it a little bit better. And now when someone disagrees or even criticizes what I believe in, I can shrug it off and even wonder compassionately about that person.

It's just going to take some falling down and getting back up. Which I'm sure you know how to do.

What if, at the end of your life, there is a questionnaire. Which box do you want to check?

☐ I made everyone happy by not expressing my passionate opinion because I didn't want to offend anyone.

☐ I expressed my opinion and it meant something big to me.

Go ahead, make everyone happy. Keep your mouth shut. Stay in your pretty box of conformity. I'll even tie up the pretty ribbon for you.

If you believe in it, it's important to you. It lives in your heart. It's a fire that cannot be put out.

Remember all those women who marched in protest to earn us the right to vote? Forgive me for getting all feminist ranting on you, but think about them for just a moment. It was the late 1910s, and there was a group of women who were absolutely freaking fed up with being second-class citizens who spoke up for the civil rights of all women. Do you think they got criticized? Do you think people disagreed with them? Oh, yes. Definitely.

They paved the way for us. Not only did they ensure we are able to vote (can you *imagine* being denied this right today?), but they set an example for us to follow: Stand up for your beliefs. It's our birthright to have our own beliefs and no one can take that away from us. And in my opinion, it's our duty as women to express them. Not with a preface of apology that looks like, "I'm sorry but . . ." but to actually say, "Here's what I think . . ."

Haters gonna hate. No matter what. For whatever reason. It's not your job to figure it out or try to convince the world to get on your side.

There is beauty and creativity in boldness.

There is beauty and creativity in boldness. Your boldness might not look like the next lady's or mine, and that's okay. Expressing your opinions and beliefs takes guts. It takes practice. It also takes some confidence. So muster up whatever you have and get out there.

And when I see you in the afterlife, I will ask you which box you checked.

CHAPTER 41

NEVER, EVER, EVER APOLOGIZE
for Who You Are

Have you ever said, "I'm sorry, but this is just how I am"?

Think about that for a minute. Would you ever say, "I'm sorry for being my true, authentic self. For acting on the personality that is embedded in my DNA."

Really?

I have two children. When I was pregnant with my second, I knew even from her activity in the womb that she was going to have a distinctly different personality than her brother. I imagined she was in there hip-hop dancing and doing somersaults while I listened to J Lo. From practically the day she was born, she's been running circles around her brother.

You were born the way you are. Yes, there is some aspect of nurture that plays a part in your personality, but for the most part, who you are is who you are. Even Lady Gaga agrees.

I love the scene in the movie, *The Family Stone*, where Luke Wilson's character says, "Everyone has a freak flag, they just don't fly it." What he's saying is that everyone has something unique about them—something they are hard-wired to do, or to be. It might be unpopular or against social norms, but so what?

It's probably something that in the past, or even now, makes you uncomfortable because it isn't "perfect" or what everyone else is doing. For instance, I have what some may call . . . a big mouth. I talk and laugh loudly, and blurt things out. I used to hate this about myself, and tried with all my might to be quieter, to be a watered-down version of what I knew I was. I tried to be what I thought our society wanted me to be. I was afraid to speak my opinions for fear of people disagreeing with me or being offended.

Does all that make me a freak? Maybe not to others, but to me, in my head, I felt like a freak. Not "normal."

So, think about your freak flag. It may come to you instantly. It may take some thinking. But here's something I know to be true: Once you recognize and embrace your freak flag, it starts to seem less . . . freaky.

Start by compiling a list of all the things you think you need to apologize for, or defend, or that make you weird. Then turn them around and ask yourself how these things have been gifts to you and what you've learned from them. For example, my "freak flag" of having a big mouth has ended up being imperative in what I do for a living, as well as in writing this book and getting it published, which was a dream of mine since I was a kid. In all honesty—as soon as I embraced this part of me, I started having better relationships, saw more success in my business, and was just generally happier.

Also, your true posse of a family, the people who truly love you . . . they don't care about your freak flag. They love you for who you are as a whole. Pinky swear. And here's some food for thought: That thing that makes you feel self-conscious, most likely . . . *no one even notices*. Since most, if not all of us, are focused on ourselves, we assume that others are watching and taking note of our freak flag, too, but truth be told everyone else is too concerned with their own problems.

I had a client who started working with me when she was twenty-seven years old. She was an introvert who preferred staying home on weekends, watching movies with her parents and younger brother. She had, a few months prior, broken up with her boyfriend who was emotionally abusive. She confided that nearly everyone around her thought she was "weird" for not wanting a relationship, not wanting to go out and party on the weekends, and the fact that she was unmarried and without children was not commonplace where she lived. Many times she felt the need to defend or be ashamed of who she was.

It's no coincidence that people who tend to apologize for who they are have low self-esteem, are constantly trying to be someone else, and have shoved themselves into a box of conformity.

It stinks in there. Get out.

When you apologize for being who you are, you're rejecting yourself. Rejecting who you naturally are, rejecting your best inner superstar. The more you reject yourself, the farther away you get from your dreams and the farther away you get from the life you were meant to live. On the other hand, *not* apologizing for who you are is about self-acceptance and fulfilling your life's purpose.

The more you reject yourself, the farther away you get from your dreams and the farther away you get from the life you were meant to live.

Flip the bird to whatever or whomever makes you feel you need to apologize for who you are. Remember, these particular people are simply dealing with their own insecurities, opinions, and projections of themselves. So, in essence, you're apologizing because someone has a different opinion than you.

Please stop.

The world needs us all to be our true, authentic selves, freak flags and all. No, we won't all get along and agree with each other all the time. But every step we get closer to our true DNA-embedded selves, the less inner suffering there is and the less we put up with things that aren't serving us. Your freak flag is yours. Love it. Wave it proudly.

CHAPTER 42

Cut Yourself Some
SLACK ALREADY

I have a tendency to put pedal to the metal. I'm a go-getter, an over-achiever, a crosser-off-of-the to-do-lister. So giving myself a break some-times looks like trying to give a cat a bath in the tub. I desperately cling to the sides, trying to get away from break time.

But here's what I've learned from my countless crash-and-burn meltdowns: I'm human, as we all are. And if I don't cut myself some slack every once in a while, life will speed by me and at the end of it I'll think, "Was this it? Did I do it right?"

The point of life is to actually *live.*

(Now I'm not here to talk to you about *carpe diem* and living in the present moment, which I think is totally a load of crap because no one can seize and sink into every moment, which just makes us all more crazy and stacks up our to-do list and makes us feel guilty . . . not to mention, write in run-on sentences. However, I digress.)

You probably already know that on our life's journey, there is tech-nically no destination. But when goals get set, ambitions get within reach, and our lives get better, sometimes the whole "destination" thing can seem like it is this dreamy place that really exists. And what's even funnier is that just when we think we're starting to get there is usually the time we get knocked on our asses.

During those times— here are some things to think about:

- **Setbacks: You're going to have them.** I would bet even Oprah calls Gayle sometimes and tells her about how she's having a negative self-talk day. Even the most evolved people still have hard times and need to work on their own stuff. No one is wrong for still having setbacks and stuff to work on, no matter how much personal growth and development hours they've clocked. So when you have a setback, try not to label it as "bad"; it just is. Fix your lipstick and forge ahead.

It's all a process. All of it. And sometimes included in that process is just having a fucking plain 'ol bad day. Or week. Every once in a while my best friend Amy and I have these conversations that Amy has lovingly nicknamed: "Shitting Glitter." We get on the phone and we bitch, moan, vent, cry, shake our fists in the air, and, well, basically have shit-fits. We listen to each other, and mostly don't try to fix it unless the other one asks. In most cases, if it's a real shit-fit, it's not about fixing it, but more about just getting it out. These don't happen very often, and when they do, we are totally aware of what is happening.

If you pretend to *never* have times like these, you're lying to yourself and to the world. Pants on fire. Feel your feelings, but if you're having a "shitting glitter" time, don't let those feelings take over your life, and, by all means, don't make big decisions during these times. Just be aware, get it out, *learn*, and move on.

- **Set reasonable goals, and then back up from those.** Then be flexible still. I get all excited come New Year's in my goal setting. I used to set lofty goals and be damned if I didn't accomplish them.

What I do now is look at the goals I've set and take them down a notch. And even then, I remember things come up and I may need to change plans.

- **Take breaks.** On days where you're so overwhelmed and don't feel like getting out of your jammies . . . don't get out of your jammies. Generally speaking, your body knows when you need a break. It's best just not to argue with the vehicle that actually houses you. I believe that when I don't give myself a break when my body asks for it—it's like throwing a drink in the face of a host who's been nothing but awesome to you.

- **Get some perspective.** When you find yourself in one of those *ohmygodlhavesomuchtodolcanttakeanymore* days, ask yourself these two questions about whatever you think it is you can't cut yourself some slack over:
  1. A year from now, will this matter? And . . .
  2. What if it just wasn't a big deal?

You may answer the first question as a yes, and that's fine (*cough bullshit*). But if you do, follow it up with figuring out how to make it not a big deal. Most of the time, it's just *deciding* it's not a big deal.

- **Keep the big picture in mind.** When we think (even subconsciously) there's a destination somewhere in life, it's also easy to lose track of the big picture. We might get tunnel vision and become fixated on productivity and business. In these moments, we tend to feel resentments: Resenting all we have to do. Resenting even the things we created at one time in the name of following our dreams. For example, maybe you started your own business, or created a workout regime. After a while, this creation seems to *need us*. Without us, everything would fall apart. In times like that, it's helpful to sit back and ask yourself what all the suffering is for. I'm not asking you to reflect on the complete and total meaning of your life, but when you get narrow vision, remind yourself what it's all really for. It's probably partially for you, for your family, for you to feel good, and maybe an act of service in there somewhere.

When you cut yourself some slack, you will probably enjoy renewed energy, reinspired vision, and reinvigorated dreams. And you never know . . . you may find yourself carpe-ing the diem. Go figure.

CHAPTER 43

WARNING:
That Perfect Body Isn't Going to Bring You Jack Shit

I've been exercising most of my life. I've belonged to a gym consistently since I was nineteen years old. Small gyms, all-women's gyms, big chain gyms, and bodybuilding gyms. In 2005, I worked corporately for the American Council on Exercise and during that time got certified as a personal trainer. I also worked for a short while training clients. I share all this stuffy resume stuff to tell you I've seen my fair share of women going after their golden ticket: the perfect body.

And I may be speaking to a brick wall here, but I'll say it anyway. This "perfect body" that we speak of—the one we see airbrushed in magazines, catalogs, billboards, commercials (yes, even commercials can be fake), and on Facebook and Pinterest—doesn't bring you anything. And I've heard the argument 1,000 times: "But it brings me confidence. I feel better about myself when my thighs are slim/ass is firm/stomach is flat/arms are tone/whatever."

And my question is . . . Why?

Why would a flat stomach bring you confidence? Why would slim hips make you feel good about yourself? And if you think it really does, I call bullshit.

You may be calling me a total bitch right now. That's fine. You might be saying, "This lady has no freaking idea what she's talking about." That's okay, too. But if you're thinking that—you're exactly the person I'm speaking to.

I speak from experience and I speak for the hundreds of girls and women I've seen over the years in gyms, in locker rooms, in classrooms, at parties, anywhere. Because I used to be that girl who thought my ticket to happiness, my ticket to love, my ticket to everything valuable, was this perfect body. Cunning and powerful . . . but baffling.

From my years of experience, I know this:

What you have going on on the outside says jack shit about what you have going on on the inside.

You can covet someone else's body, pick yours apart, or even hate your own, but having that outside package you so badly want will give you nothing but a false sense of happiness. An empty prize. Oh, it may very well make you happy for a very short time. You may have had a goal to lose weight or get to a certain size and you got there. But if you're relying on that weight or size to bring you the happiness and fulfillment you're missing, you're in for a major disappointment, my friend.

Instead, work on your inside first. Try facing your demons, because lord knows you have them. We all do. Try coping in ways that feed your soul instead of coping by hustling and scrambling to look perfect for everyone else and this voice in your head. Because the people who really care what your body looks like should not be worth a shit to you.

Don't know where to start? Start here:

Question: What are you afraid might happen if you don't have that perfect body?

Afraid someone might not love you? Afraid you aren't worthy? What is it?

Truth: You are worthy of love no matter what your body looks like.

★

Question: What are you not facing while you're so busy on your quest for that perfect body? What's going on in your life that needs your immediate attention that you're ignoring? Your marriage or relationships? Your job that sucks? Your lack of self-love or self-esteem? What?

Truth: Those last five pounds are not the answer. Another workout isn't the answer. *Your* attention to your life is the answer.

★

Question: How do you cope with life's hard times? (And don't act like you don't have any!) How do you feel your feelings?

Truth: If you numb your feelings or go unconscious when you don't want to feel something, not only will it not go away, it will get worse. You need to *feel* your feelings. Break down in a crying heap if you need to. Be vulnerable. Be messy. Be imperfect. Be a train wreck.

★

And here's one last truth: If and when you get to a place where you've worked for and achieved this "perfect body," there will always be something else. Something else that isn't right about your outside appearance. And you'll try to fix that, too. And while you're trying to fix that, there is something inside you that is dying for your attention. Please don't spend another day lying to yourself thinking this "perfect body" is the answer to your problems. Please don't spend another night in bed thinking, "What is *wrong* with me?" Please don't spend another day criticizing yourself and wishing your body were different. Doing this is like kicking your soul's ass.

Every bit of you is perfect, unique, and amazing. So many people love and adore you to pieces just the way you are. Start believing them.

CHAPTER 44

YOU + GRATITUDE
= Always Enough

The term "gratitude" gets thrown around a lot lately. It's like the trendy personal development topic du jour. And I really only have one thing to say about that:

Hell yes.

I have yet to meet a person who lives her life in complete joy, fulfillment, and abundance but doesn't practice gratitude. If there was only one thing in my life I was able to do in terms of personal development, it would hands down be gratitude. It is my go-to tool to make me feel better any time, in any situation. And every time I feel like things aren't going well in my life and I don't generally feel good mentally, emotionally, or spiritually, I realize that I've slacked off on my gratitude practice. Getting back to gratitude always helps.

I remember the moment gratitude changed my life. I had just found out my boyfriend of nine months had not only cheated on me but had lied about everything in our relationship. I was lying on the floor of my packed-up bedroom in the fetal position (said boyfriend and

I were going to move in together so I had gotten out of my apartment lease and quit my awesome job), sobbing my eyes out. I thought I had hit rock bottom ten months before when my marriage ended, but this was below rock bottom. I felt like a loser. I could see no light at the end of the tunnel and I was officially hopeless.

I remembered hearing about gratitude and that it could help. I was desperate. Begrudgingly, I got out a piece of paper and wrote down ten things I was grateful for at that moment. Things such as physical health, my education, my family, and the clothes on my back. That was the first step of many I took to healing and becoming the woman I am today, way on the other side. That's how powerful gratitude can be.

Let's start from the beginning. What are the benefits of being grateful, anyway?

- Many scientific studies show that people who practice gratitude regularly are happier and experience less bouts of depression.
- Gratitude brings humility. Ain't nothing wrong with being humble, right?
- Gratitude opens our hearts, brings us more awareness, and opens us up to give more love and receive more love. And, after all, that's what we're here for, y'all.
- Practicing gratitude can attract *more* of the things you are grateful for into your life.
- Gratitude makes everything we are enough and everything we have enough.

Practicing gratitude by no means has to be complicated or involved. The most common exercise is listing what you're grateful for every morning or night. I'd like to take it a step further and suggest more ways to embrace gratitude. But, the first thing you need to do is *commit to the practice.* If you've never tried this, commit to at least thirty days of gratitude.

1. First up is the actual practice. Create a daily ritual where you write down your gratitudes. Commit to doing it a certain time of day— maybe it's while you drink your morning coffee, or while you exercise, or first thing when you get to work. Write at least three things, but if you have more, by all means write them down. While it's fine to have repeats day after day, try your best to think of new things to be grateful for. I often challenge my clients to make a list of 100 things.

2. Now for the coming attractions. It's easy to quickly take inventory of what you have now, the obvious ones, for example: health, happiness, home, and loved ones. Next, try to add on things that you are grateful that are *coming to you.* If you're in a rough place, be grateful now that soon you will be on the other side of this. If you know exactly what you want, be grateful for the fact that it's on its way.

3. Try this one on for size: Practice gratitude for the hard stuff. Instead of thinking of difficult situations or decisions you've made and regret and beating yourself up for it, try thinking about how that situation has made you a better you. What did you learn from it? How will it shape you going forward? What are you grateful it showed you?

4. Another way to practice gratitude is to specifically thank people who aren't expecting it. Write a letter to your parents. E-mail a former teacher. Put a Post-It in your mailbox for your letter carrier. Send a postcard to your spouse's work. Text your kids' teachers and tell them thanks for what they do. With all the business of life, we often forget and take for granted the people we love and appreciate the most. Don't let that happen.

5. Finally, when you're out at places like the grocery store or getting a cup of coffee, thank the person who helped you and look him or her in the eye when you do so. Connecting on a human level and expressing gratitude at the same time is powerful.

If you have children, teaching them the practice of gratitude is a major life lesson they can take with them for the rest of their lives. In our house at the dinner table we do, "What makes you happy?" We started this when our kids were five and three years old, so to make it age appropriate we made the question simple. Of course, my son started out saying what made him happy were things like Legos and fire trucks, but I'll never forget the second day when he said, "You! You and daddy make me happy!"

Don't stop once you start seeing results. Gratitude picks up momentum and just keeps getting better with time.

CHAPTER 45

CREATE
a Tribe of Badasses

Like attracts like. It's science. If you feel great about yourself, you'll attract other people who feel great about themselves.

Surround yourself with assholes, and you're in for a shitty life.

As human beings, we are wired for connection with other human beings. It's unnatural to be alone all the time. Even Maslow's Hierarchy of Needs states that humans require belonging and love. I believe people are happier when they have people in their lives who bring out their best attributes. Show me a person who truly enjoys being with someone who criticizes and points out his or her flaws. You can't.

Right now, take a look around you. If you can't figure out why you're unhappy, why you keep picking the same jerks to be in relationships with, or why crappy things keep happening to you, take inventory of the key players in your life. You might have a couple of gems. But you might also have a few assholes floating around that are bringing you down.

You know that phrase, "Misery loves company"? The jerks in your life are actually *trying* to bring you down. It's like their extracurricular activity.

And if you happen to be one of those assholes I speak of, you're going to need to do some inner work before you can attract the right people. Get some therapy. Read this book again and again. Work on your stuff.

You might be at a point in your life when you're surrounding yourself with the people you think you "should" be around instead of the people you want to be around. Maybe they're old friends (if so, see Chapter 16). Maybe it's the cool, mysterious crowd. Either way, why are you spending your precious time and energy with them? History? Coolness factor? You need to be around people who bring value and respect to your life. If your current crowd isn't doing that, it's time to reassess.

If you're ready to create your tribe—the group of wonderful people in your life—here are some ways to do it:

1. **Figure out *who* you want in your tribe and why.** What kind of people do you admire and want to emulate? What kind of attributes do they have? Are they kind, funny, do they have jobs? Be specific. Who is someone, living or otherwise, that you love? Was it your grandmother? If so, why? And if you answer, "I love and admire Channing Tatum because he's hot," that's not the type of answer I'm looking for. Think about intrinsic qualities you want for yourself and admire in others.

2. **Listen to your gut instincts.** Pay attention to how you react to people. If it's a first meeting, are you drawn to them even though you can't explain why? What is it about their essence or energy that draws you to them?

3. **Reinforce relationships with the great people you already know.** Do you have people already in your life who you want to strengthen the bonds with? Take action and plan something with

them. Focus on things that you know you both like, such as book clubs, getting tattoos, meeting for coffee, shopping at thrift stores, etc. You could even create rituals such as meeting for breakfast the last Friday of every month.

4. **Embrace virtual connections.** Social media has made it so easy for us to connect, even if it's on a virtual level. Search for people or groups on Yahoo!, Facebook, or Twitter who share the same interests and passions you do. When you get to know people there, it's pretty easy to eventually create an in-person meet-up if you want.

When you create this tribe of badasses for yourself, I guarantee you will see a shift. It won't happen overnight, but you will see things change. It's hard to surround yourself with people that are self-loving and authentic and not be that type of person yourself.

Bottom line: Don't wait for your tribe to come to you. You may be waiting around forever. Be proactive in your efforts to create your tribe. Even if you're a shy, introverted type, you can still find ways to create the key players in your life that you want in ways that feel comfortable to you.

CHAPTER 46

CLOSURE Is Overrated

How many times have you said, "I really need to get some closure around this" when speaking in terms of a relationship or event that has happened? You want to remove the feelings of heaviness that are probably weighing on you and affecting your day-to-day life. It's like walking around with a wedgie you can't pick. You're uncomfortable and no amount of shifting around is helping. You want the relief.

Closure is defined as "bringing to an end" and "the act of closing," but it can mean different things for different people. It might mean you need to tell an ex exactly what you think of him or your relationship, maybe you need to return his favorite college sweatshirt, or it might mean you need to tell him to screw off, or that deep down you really want to keep in touch.

Let's say a relationship has ended. It's over and that may suck. What I think is a myth around this topic is the notion that you can have one conversation over coffee, hug it out, and get "closure." As if those elusive last words are what bring relief and tie it all up with a pretty bow.

Truth: It doesn't.

Sure, there might be some things you need to say, to clear up. Maybe you need to offer a much needed apology and ask for forgiveness.

But where I think this myth of closure messes with people is when they assume that some specific action will heal their wounds. And the search for this imaginary action can cause even more grief.

When my first marriage ended, I kept feeling like if I had one more conversation with my ex-husband I would feel better. If I told him one more time how hurt I was, or apologized for anything I had done in our relationship, that would be closure for me. Somewhere along my quest for all of this I realized I just wanted the pain to go away. I wanted the event to go away. I wanted to *not* be divorced, alone, and have to start over. And the reality was nothing was going to change that. Closure wasn't going to bring all of that for me. Nothing was going to heal me except me.

For a while after we split, we did keep having conversations. Conversations that revolved around what happened to us. Apologies, asking for forgiveness, updates on how our lives were without each other in it. If I could paint the picture of what I thought closure looked like, that was it.

After all that, what I came to realize was there was nothing either of us could say to change what happened. We were done. The circumstances of that breakup were painful. No words, no apologies, no amount of tears were going to change that or make it go away. I needed to either let it all go, or be okay with the fact that what happened, happened. Or both.

I've heard it often, "I never got any closure." And then the person desperately tries to contact the person, or beats him or herself up to a pulp because there is no way to get it.

The definition of closure you're looking for may never, ever happen. Your only job is to create the closure you need in order to feel peace and love for yourself.

You can't change the past, ever. You can't make the other person feel a certain way. You can't make them accept your apology, or listen to you if they don't want to. And even if they do listen, remember, they may not react as you want. You probably have this fantasy in your head of how the conversation would go (don't tell me you've never scripted it), complete with background music. But this isn't the movies.

What might help are a few small steps in the positive direction that will add up to a bigger amount of healing. Here are some suggestions:

- Write a letter with no intention of sending it. Without the intention of the other person reading it, you're more likely to write it for you. Tell the other person exactly how you feel. Don't hold back. When you're done, keep it in a safe place, or if you're into rituals, do something symbolic with the letter.
- Write out your whole story. You can even get creative here and make it a poem, a play, or whatever you want. The point again is to get it all out and be able to read it back to hopefully gain healing and new perspective.
- Look into energy healing. I believe that when a relationship ends, many times the energy from the relationship still lives inside of us. If you're open to that sort of thing, it can be very healing.
- Ask yourself what is it that you really need from this "closure"? Is it to forgive yourself for a mistake you made in the relationship? Something you said or did?

Do yourself a favor. Accept that what is done is done. Let go. *You* are in complete control of your own closure in any situation. *You* get to decide if you want to torture yourself forever and be a victim of your "unclosed" circumstance, or do whatever you can to create your own peace in your heart.

So, which do you want?

CHAPTER 47

LIFE BALANCE
Is a Crock of Shit

I get this question all the time: "How do I find life balance?" I used to freak out when my coaching clients would ask me to coach them on this, because *I had no freakin' clue!* I myself was constantly searching for it, thinking other women had figured out this "life balance" thing, and surely I was a failure at life, motherhood, marriage, and everything else because I did not know how to do it. I was chasing an elusive unicorn riding on a double rainbow and I was getting rather tired.

Throw in a couple cups of coffee with that thought stream and I was sure to have a complete and total freak-out.

Then, one day, I was reading Danielle LaPorte's blog and she said there is no such thing as life balance. That the quest for life balance is actually bringing us more stress and that we can never get it right.

I fainted.

Not really, but it was the answer I had been looking for and I could not agree more with Ms. LaPorte. Here's the thing: I don't know *any woman* that has life balance 100 percent of the time. And those who say they do are either high on Valium or lying to your face.

We are constantly inundated with things to do. Things we "should" do. Things we need to do to be evolved, Zen, and mellowed out. We watch Oprah and aimlessly search our Facebook news feed for the answers to our problems.

The truth is, somewhere along they way, we're all going to fall short—in our job, our marriage and relationships, as parents, and as friends. And with this comes feelings of guilt, and not being enough. Yet at the same time, trying to be all things to all people while creating balance within all of it is a sure-fire way to feel like a failure.

So we can accept that a true specific definition of life balance doesn't exist and just do the best we can, or we can keep trying to look for this proverbial unicorn on the double rainbow and always come up short.

Your choice.

Several years ago, I had a mentor who told me she looks at life balance using the metaphor of a cattle dog herding its cattle. All the cows are moving along for a while in order, and then one or two veer off in another direction. The herding dog runs out to nip the outlying cows and gets them back on track. This happens several times and it's just the nature of the herd. The dog really never knows which cow will run off course or when, but he knows it's his job to get things back in order so that the entire herd stays safe. It's never a perfect herd going in one smooth direction.

I think our lives aren't that much different than these cows and dogs (nice metaphor, huh?). Especially if you're a mom who leads your family, but even if you're not, chances are you can relate to this. I think once we can let go of life balance needing to look a certain way, therein lies the first step to freedom.

Before I begin the how, for the record, I'd like to change the term "life balance" to "striving for some sort of sanity in this mad, mad world." There, that feels better.

Let's go over some ways to make sure you're in a place of "doing the best you can," shall we? That way, you can redefine what life balance is for you, remain flexible within that definition, and go on your merry way.

1. Go to Chapter 4 and review your list of values. If you're not honoring most of them on at least a minimal effort, you're bound to feel completely lost and perhaps in crisis. Check those values, sister. And by the same token, revisit your nonnegotiables (Chapter 13). Is exercise a nonnegotiable you haven't done and made the excuse "I don't have time"? Nonnegotiables are just that: *non*-negotiable. Nothing is going to be "balanced" or "sane" if you're not honoring your values or getting your nonnegotiables.

2. Notice if you're comparing your life to someone else's. Chances are, what you're comparing your life to isn't reality, but what you see on the outside. You might see glimpses of people's herds going along smoothly, and somewhere you assume that's the way it always is for them. Truth: it's not. So notice if you find yourself lost in someone's pictures of their smiling kids, their vacation, their awards, and all the glowing, fabulous times.

3. Determine what exactly life balance looks and feels like to you. And when you're clear on that definition, make room for flexibility and some craziness sometimes. Is it one day a week of nothing on your schedule? If so, keep it sacred with no exceptions (looks like it just became a nonnegotiable!). Is it healthy and open communication with your husband? Make sure he's on board. These things might be easy to forget because they're so basic and foundational, right in front of our noses.

And remember, girls—we're all struggling and flailing sometimes. Let's all agree to give ourselves and each other a break when it comes to this myth of life balance.

CHAPTER 48

FAIL More Often

Did you cringe a little when you read that chapter title? Don't worry; I cringed a little when I wrote it.

The word "fail" is *the* four-letter "f word" to many. It's painful, ugly, humiliating, and just unacceptable. Ask any out-of-control dad at his kid's Pop Warner football game and he'll tell you so. And watch out for the vein on his forehead; it's about to burst.

And it's not like I'm the first person to talk about this. The Internet is riddled with articles about how important failure is for us. Psychologists, scholars, and teachers talk about this regularly. But still, there is something inside us all that has a really hard time with failure. I believe for women, perfectionism and our outward appearance and perception of others often fuels our fear of failure, which is tragic if you think about it. We're afraid to try something new because we fear people's opinions of us. When, in reality, "those people" are probably just as afraid themselves and/or perhaps don't really care as much as we think they do.

Sort of ridiculous, don't you think?

Here's the good news: everyone has failed. Whether it's been on a test, a relationship, a business venture, a new idea, Rollerblading, trying to bring thong leotards back in style, anything at all. Everyone takes risks and gambles every day; it's a part of life. And sometimes it doesn't work out.

Think about a specific situation where you've failed. How do you tell the story about it? For instance, let's say you started a business, used your savings to fund it, and ended up having to close it. When you tell someone about it, do you say, "My business went under, I lost everything, and it sucked. I wish I would have never started it. It was a stupid decision." Or, do you say, "Unfortunately, I had to close the business. I learned *so* much from the experience and loved it."

You get to choose how not only you look at the situation, but how you relay the story to others. When you think about or talk about your failure, how does it make you feel? If it makes you feel shitty—and by now you should know what I'm about to say—it's time to recreate your thoughts about the situation. You have total and complete control over those thoughts and how they create your feelings.

The hard truth is that if you haven't failed, you haven't tried hard enough. And if you haven't tried hard enough, you're playing small. And if you're playing small, that's your true failure.

When you think of your favorite athlete, author, or actor, do you think about how many times he or she has failed? No, you think about how awesome you think he or she is.

When you're headed out to whatever the afterlife is, here on earth no one will talk about how many times you failed when you were living. No one will give a shit that it didn't work out with knitting that blanket or starting that business or making a soufflé. No, they'll think about and talk about how fantastic you were. But how will they know about how awesome you are if you spend your life playing small in fear of failure?

I meet women all the time who are afraid of doing something they want because they are afraid of failing at it. Many of them think they need to get to a place of fearlessness before they take action.

Here's a secret: I hate the word "fearless." I think it's bullshit. I have yet to meet a person who is completely absent of fear. We all have it in varying degrees. It's just that some of us choose to push through it and others don't. You choose the group you're in.

In the movie *Three Kings*, George Clooney's character Archie says, "The way it works is, you do the thing you're scared shitless of, and you get the courage *after* you do it, not before you do it." And I totally believe this to be true. So, if it is true, if we get the courage afterwards to do that thing we're scared shitless of, that thing we're afraid of failing at, would that change the way you did things? What if I told you that *everyone* you think is courageous had found their courage *after* they took action? Would that give you a push?

The only failure is not trying. It's a true failure to allow your inner critic to live your life and make your decisions. It's a true failure to play small and safe for fear of looking bad to everyone else.

And you're way too good for that.

CHAPTER 49

EXERCISE
Should Not Be Corporal Punishment

I could not write this book without talking about this.

If you and exercise are BFFs, feel free to skip this chapter, but if you're like most people on this planet, you're not a big fan of exercise and wish you were.

There are physiological reasons you may not like exercise that for the sake of this chapter I won't get into (i.e., *bor-ing*). But, for the love of God, please don't feel that exercise has to be punishment. It's no surprise many people hate exercise because it's probably been used as a means of punishment either from yourself, coaches, phys ed teachers, doctors, or parents. And please, please, don't punish yourself with exercise for not following through with your diet. You don't need to be punished for anything, *especially* not that.

The bottom line is human bodies are meant to be in motion. Physically and biologically, we haven't evolved that much from thousands of years ago (except for being overly hairy . . . which is good, right?) when humans used to exercise just to survive. And it wasn't even *exercise*. It was just *moving*. So what if we started there? Instead of thinking of it as exercise, or calling it that, what if you just looked at it from the perspective of *movement*. Don't worry about calories burned, or time, or which workout outfit makes you look skinnier.

The big, gigantic point here is to do what feels good to you. And I have to call bullshit if you say nothing does. If you can get your ass out of bed in the morning and walk to the coffee maker, you can muster up the energy to move and play.

And maybe there's something you want to do that's different. Maybe you're a guy who wants to do Zumba, or a girl who wants to box. Or try trapeze. Are you the kind of person who can't hear an up-beat ringtone on a phone without shaking your booty? Then just dance in your house, in your car, while getting dressed, anywhere. Whatever you do to move your body doesn't have to look like exercise. Some people loathe the gym. That's fine, just find another way.

When I was buying roller skates several months ago for roller derby a woman came into the store who looked like she was in her mid to late sixties. She was also buying roller skates. We started talking and she told me she loves to exercise, but was tired of walking. She's always loved roller-skating as a young girl and feels in her heart that she wants to skate again. She said she's been having dreams about skating, so she came in to buy herself some skates for her birthday.

What a badass lady.

After we'd been talking for a few minutes, I told her I thought she was awesome for skating again, for doing something she felt in her heart. She looked relieved and said, "I really thought I would come in here and be laughed at for being a grandma who wanted to skate for exercise."

It got me thinking . . . how many people out there are doing exercises they don't want to do because they think they "should," or because the thing they really want to do, they're afraid to. I can't tell you how many people I meet that start running for exercise and tell me they hate it. If you hate running, don't do it. If you think yoga is the most boring thing ever, stop. Find something else. If necessary, try twenty different ways to exercise until you find the one you love. Or at least like better than the one you hate. It's like dating. Not the right one? Look for another.

I'll ask again—at the end of your life, are you going to look back and like the fact that you spent hundreds of hours doing an activity that you didn't like?

Sign up for unhappy activities and you'll get that: unhappy activities. Which will equal unhappiness, self-sabotage, resentment, panties in a wad . . . you get the picture.

In addition to committing to not punishing yourself with exercise, renaming it to "movement," and stepping out of the box and trying what you want, here are some more tips:

- **Get a partner.** Accountability buddies are the best thing since Chuck Norris (bonus points if you can get Chuck Norris to *be* your accountability buddy). Set *realistic* goals with each other, design how you each want to be held accountable, and stick to it.
- **Celebrate like crazy over your accomplishments.** Even if it's just starting each workout. Starting and creating the habit can be the hardest part, so even if you only get a five-minute workout in, it's a victory!
- **Take turtle steps.** Too much too soon can lead to feeling overwhelmed, injury, burnout, even boredom. Simple soreness can make you quit. Sometimes baby steps are too big, so try turtle steps.

P.S. Kegels *do* count as exercise, but don't make it your only one.

CHAPTER 50

Find Some Kind of
SPIRITUALITY

This chapter may be a bit controversial. You may love it or hate it.

A confession: I'm married to a nonbeliever. Sometimes I wonder when the day comes to meet my Maker and I'm standing before him, will he say, "Great job on your life! But . . . marrying a nonbeliever? What the hell was that about?"

Point being that I don't judge what anyone believes about spirituality. Most of us are praying to the same God in my opinion, so I choose not to argue. My husband and I have discussions about what is really "out there" after death. He firmly believes in "the big bang theory" and when we die, we die. There is nothing else.

I, on the other hand, think differently, partly because I grew up in a Christian home, but mostly because I choose to believe there is something out there greater than me. I believe that there is something out there that gives me the wisdom I ask for. Something that gives me pretty much everything I ask for, when the time is right and I am ready to receive it. And I'll tell you what—everything I've learned in the last seven years, the heart and soul I've poured into this book and into my business, my marriage, parenting, and everything, I know has been handed down to be from a Higher Power.

In the most difficult times in my life—my parents' divorce, my own divorce, my sobriety (more on that next), and more—I felt lost, hopeless, and desperate. In those moments, I turned to my spirituality. It was essential in me being able to let *everything* go, to let go of pain and suffering and to heal.

Now, I really don't care what or who you believe in or don't believe in. **The bottom line is I think it's imperative for people to be able to give up control.** To be able to give away their pain.

A few days after I found out my ex-husband was having an affair and that he wanted a divorce, my mom and stepdad came to stay with me from out of state in my little apartment. I came home from work one day to find out my mom had been on a walk, tripped and fell, and had badly scraped up her face in the street. She wasn't badly hurt, but the sight of her with the side of her face looking like hamburger meat was too much to bear at that moment. I shooed them out, sent them back home to get better, and closed the door. I then fell to my knees and cried.

I said out loud: "I don't know what is in store for me . . . but I know this isn't it. I *cannot* take this pain and suffering. My heart cannot bear anymore. Please help and take some of it." My life didn't magically change at that moment. No clouds parted. No lightning struck. But what did happen was my spirit shifted. I felt hope that I didn't have to live like that forever. That something better and bigger was planned for me. All I had to do was stay hopeful instead of hopeless, even if it was just a slight tip of the scale in the direction of hope.

In times like those, the power in believing there is something out there bigger than ourselves, looking out for us, can be life changing. Call it angels, spirits, God, the Universe, whatever you want. There is something out there made entirely of love.

And if you look at it that way—a giant energy of love that is looking out for you—isn't that the best thing ever?

I'll admit I tend to be the type of person who calls on my spirituality when I'm reaching for my parachute. Not just reaching for my parachute, but also yelling, *"Shit! Shit! Heeeelp!"* I do practice gratitude on a regular basis, but I could really use some sprucing up of my everyday practice of spirituality. The thing I've learned is that spirituality doesn't have to look a certain way for anyone. I know even the term "spirituality" makes people uncomfortable, and "religion" makes others want to run and hide. So call it what you want. Call it love, unearthly presence, grace, essential nature, whatever makes you feel good. Because in case you haven't gotten the message yet . . . what makes you feel good about something is generally good for you.

I'm not asking you to adopt any kind of religion if you don't want it. All I'm asking is for you to find some place in your life where you can give up control, pain, angst, hopelessness, desperation, stress, and anything else that makes you feel like you're drowning.

Because anything that makes your life more peaceful and easier is just that much more energy you have to live your kick-ass life.

Truth.

CHAPTER 51

OWN UP
to What You Use to Numb Your Feelings

I wouldn't be writing this chapter if I weren't the former mayor of NumbYourFeelings Town. I have been addicted in varying degrees to relationships, shopping, the scale, exercise, perfection, control, and alcohol. It wasn't until I got sober in 2011 that I fully realized that I was using so many different things to numb my feelings . . . and jumping from one thing to the next like I was doing some kind of plyometrics workout.

The first thing I want to say is: If you numb your feelings, you're normal. I'm not saying it's okay, but noticing and admitting is the first step.

Some of you may not be able to relate because you don't have addictive behaviors like many of us. But consider that if you are constantly trying to change the way you feel by using something outside of you, you might be addicted to it.

If you're stressed, upset, frustrated, angry, lonely, or sad, do you pour yourself a drink to feel better? Or do you binge eat? Or look for love/sex/dates from others? Or even do things like sleep, gossip, or procrastinate?

Or do you just sit with your feelings and let them wash over you? If that seems like a completely foreign and scary concept to you, read on.

Society teaches us that certain feelings are "bad," such as desperation, fury, jealousy. Even sadness gets a bad rap. Society also dictates that we should or shouldn't feel certain ways. Or that we should as quickly as possible change our feelings to "better" ones.

Should, should, should, *shitty*.

I also think what perpetuates numbing behaviors is other people telling us how to feel. How many times have you heard, "Don't feel bad!" or, "Don't cry . . . it's not that awful, and it could be worse." And then you feel worse because your feelings have just been invalidated. The truth here is when people tell you something like this, their words have nothing to do with you, only them. It makes *them* uncomfortable to see you in pain. They want the hard feelings to go away, for happiness to come back. Their intentions are good, but many times it can make you actually feel worse and/or you do whatever you can to not feel the very real feelings that are happening inside you.

One of my clients had been working with me for many months. We would meet about once a month for check-ins. In one session, she told me she was facing some stress at work, which was causing her anxiety, and she was noticing some of her old negative thoughts coming back. She was worried she would go all the way back to the "way she was before" if she didn't immediately change and wanted me to help her. What she wanted was to, in her words, "make those feelings go away." I asked her, "Sure, we can work on this . . . but what if you just let yourself be and feel whatever you're feeling instead of resisting and fighting it? What do you think?" And she responded with one word: Relief.

What if . . .

- Our feelings were just perfect for us?
- None of our feelings were "bad" or "wrong"?
- Feeling the more difficult feelings was just part of being human?
- Feeling all of our feelings was what made us even more awesome?
- We could learn more about our world and ourselves by feeling all of our feelings?
- **What if feelings, all of them, just weren't a big deal?**

Remember Chapter 1 where I said you have a choice when it come to your feelings? You can choose to feel your feelings or not. But when you numb them, it doesn't mean you erase them. They still exist.

I know firsthand that addiction can be a very real thing, and if you think it might be affecting you, please get professional help. My intention for this chapter is for you to notice what you're doing when you're trying to run away from your feelings. The thing is, you can't unknow what you already know when it comes to self-realizations. When you're pretty sure (or are absolutely positive) some of your behaviors aren't serving you, or might be harming you, it becomes really hard to push that realization away. Bottom line: I'm asking you to get really honest with yourself about what's going on.

Sometimes we don't even know what it is that we're trying to numb. Yes, sometimes it's plainly obvious. But if you don't know, the best way to find out what you're trying to numb is to stop numbing for three days. When you think of reaching for a drink, a pill, food, whatever, ask yourself what you're feeling. What are you trying to change? What are you running away from? What is making you uncomfortable?

And just sit with it. Whatever it is, know that you are not wrong. There is nothing wrong with you for what you are feeling. Keep trying the three-day challenge until you can identify what you need help with and find the appropriate help for it.

CHAPTER 52

KNOW
This Is Exactly Where
You Are Supposed to Be

I can't remember the first time I heard, "This is exactly where you're supposed to be," but I know it was when I was having a hard time with some crisis. I distinctly remember hating those words and probably told the person that told me that to eff off. I thought it was easy for that person to tell me those words and I was not sure what I was supposed to do with that information.

And here's what I've learned: Whether you're struggling through a difficult time, or enjoying a great, positive one—these moments are all critical to the path you're on, whether you love them or hate them. The optimal word here is . . .

Trust.

Trust that the Universe has your back. Trust that you were meant for and are capable of greatness. Trust that if you aren't where you want to be right now, something wonderful is about to happen. And trust that you have the strength and patience to persevere. Because the only way out . . . is through.

Trust that you were meant for and are capable of greatness.

You might be in a place of low self-esteem, lack of confidence, and stuck in comparing yourself to others. Trust that where you are right now will eventually be a place that you look back on and see how far you've come.

You might be hurting from a breakup. Trust that the situation will be a huge learning experience. You'll look back and be able to see clearly what you want and don't want in your next relationship. You can own what you need to improve on and what you'll tolerate. Eventually.

Or you might be in grief. I've heard that therapists call grief the "healing feeling" and I believe this to be true. Is it hard and sucky? Yes. And sometimes each day seems to drag on like you're carrying a 200-pound sack of potatoes in your heart. Trust that grief will heal you eventually.

Maybe you're lost in an addiction. Addicted to food, lost in an eating disorder, alcohol, drugs, love/sex/relationships, shopping, or anything. It might feel like there's no way out, no light at the end of the tunnel. Trust that this experience has the vast capacity to make you well . . . eventually.

Perhaps you're lost about what your purpose is. You feel time ticking by and that most other people have it figured out . . . everyone except you. Trust that maybe instead of you finding your purpose, your purpose will find you eventually.

In coaching, I often ask my clients, "What's perfect about this moment?" and the truth is—sometimes that question is so jarring, it makes people feel panicked, as if they *have* to think of something "perfect" in what feels like a very imperfect moment.

If finding something "perfect" is too overwhelming, ask yourself what's *not* wrong with this moment or situation. Focus on that. Allow yourself to settle into bits and pieces that just might be little stepping-stones toward healing. Tiny bread crumbs of your path that are taking you to your biggest, highest most kick-ass self.

Mama Gena, author of "Mama Gena's School of Womanly Arts," says, *"Decide that wherever you are is the right place to be."* The keyword here being *decide*. Decide, decide, decide. I'm a true believer that whatever we resist, persists. If you are dealing with a difficult situation and are desperately trying to escape and run away . . . try *deciding* that wherever you are is the right place to be.

And if nothing else, there's always the option of standing still right now, wherever you are. What if today, or even this week, this month, and this year you weren't supposed to be one bit smarter, more evolved, more present, more courageous, better, or faster at anything. That what is actually the absolute best thing for you is to be absolutely still.

And yeah, your best self and your kick-ass life are still out there. Don't worry; they'll wait for you. And all your trips, falls, wrong turns, and days where you stand still are part of what you'll need to get there. Eventually.

Index